Walking in Darkness, Walking in Light

A Tragic Yet Inspirational Story of Hope and Redemption Where There Should Be None

By Jeffrey A. Sinnott

DORRANCE
PUBLISHING CO
EST. 1920
PITTSBURGH, PENNSYLVANIA 15238

Dorrance Publishing Co
585 Alpha Drive
Pittsburgh, PA 15238
Visit our website at *www.dorrancebookstore.com*

ISBN: 979-8-88729-386-8
eISBN: 979-8-88729-886-3

Table of Contents

Chapter 1

The Family

On February 1, 1962, I was born in the city of Worcester, Massachusetts, to Joseph and Barbara Sinnott (Mack). It was a cold New England day. Growing up in Worcester in the 1960s as a white kid from a two-parent home in a middle class to upper middle-class neighborhood should have been easy, but life seldom turns out as expected.

It has taken me years to figure out why I turned out the way I did. For the reader to understand, it is necessary to introduce the members of my family and the environment in which I grew up. It is also important to give you an overview of my circumstances as an adult and the influences I was exposed to in life.

Dad

My father, Joseph Sinnott, was a good but flawed man. By that I mean he paid the bills, taught me right from wrong, wanted the best for me and for the family, and tried to be a good and honest person. Dad taught us about nature, gun safety, geology, and to be wary of strangers. He also taught each of us how to drive years before we were legally able to do so.

The flaws were that he was an active alcoholic who worked all the time and seldom had time for his children. He relegated the raising of the family to my mother. That was a bad decision on his part, but that was also the custom of the times. Dad went to work, and Mom stayed home.

I don't know if my mom and dad ever loved each other, or if they just ended up together because that was what was expected of them in the 1950s. My father always seemed like a street kid that had done well and married up. He came from very humble Irish-American roots. On the other hand, Mom came from a well-to-do Lithuanian family and was a snobby girl who married down. I believe that in their marriage my dad resented my mom's ambition and that she resented his lack of ambition. This was a major cause of disagreement between them.

During my early years, Dad had three jobs. He started his own business (Sinnott Geological Engineering) in which he did test borings and geological surveys to determine where building should be built or even to find gas/oil. He also taught Geology at the prestigious Clark University in Worcester, Massachusetts. Eventually, he became the state geologist for the State of Massachusetts. My father would bring me to work with him at Clark University when he didn't have classes and let me check out their fossils - of which they had an extensive collection. From trilobites to mastodons, dinosaur footprints to my favorite of all, the saber tooth tiger skull. He spent the entire second half of his life working for the state and found fulfillment in that job. It provided opportunities to assist with a variety of projects, such as working on the pirate ship, the Whydah, which was found off Cape Cod. That job also allowed him to be an independent amateur archaeologist during his free time for which he was credited with finding a lost Native American culture in western Massachusetts. Their culture was known for carving stone faces into the rocks. Dad was happy doing this type of work and was satisfied with his place in life. Mom, however, thought he should aspire to do better. "Why don't you apply for a better paying job with a scientific research company?" she suggested. But he was not inclined to look for other work as he was happy where he was.

The best memories I have of him is when he used to pile all the kids into the car on Sunday mornings as he put the top down on the convertible. We could all stand up in the car and let the wind blow through our hair. This was in the days when police officers wouldn't pull you over for child endangerment with several unconstrained kids in the car. We would drive out to the town of Upton where my dad co-owned 23 acres. There, we could run, swim, fish and explore the woods all day looking for turtles, snakes, or deer.

During each visit at the end of the day, we would stop by a little country store and buy candy or Yahoos (a chocolate milk drink), which we loved so much. Each Sunday morning would end the same way, with all the kids piling back into his white Buick with the red interior as Dad listened to Johnny Cash and tapped out of time to the Sunday morning radio station.

My dad was a tall, balding man who liked science and nature. He always looked serious because he didn't smile much. Dad would teach us about nature and life. If he could do so simply by walking in the woods alongside a pond, out in the country, or at his friend's house who had a pig farm, all the better. The man who owned the pig farm was Arnie Bjorklund. Dad would take us to the farm, and as they sat inside the farmhouse, he would encourage us to drive up and down the dirt road unsupervised. We would chase the baby piglets and get scared when the sow would jump up and confront us from her pen. We learned about sex by watching the animals. We learned where meat comes from, and about death by watching Arnie slaughter a pig by shooting the pig in the head, and then slicing its throat as it hung upside down by its hooves. His wife Maya would then catch the draining blood in a pot and beat it with a whisk, so that she could make blood sausage. That was the end of sausage for me. Then they would gut it and boil the hair off.

I don't remember a lot of dialogue with my dad, but I do remember a few words of advice. The first was "Don't tell your mother about this" when he didn't want her to know something of which she might not approve such as shooting at her city council signs which had her picture on them. The second was, "Don't marry the town whore." Good advice! Dad didn't say a lot and when he said "Barbara," we knew that meant they would discuss a sensitive topic later and not in front of us kids. The kids were never told anything about health, finances, or making good decisions.

Mom

My relationship with my mother was extremely complicated. I have both loved her and hated her in equal measure. As a child, I mostly hated her because I never felt loved or wanted by her and felt she resented me and that I was an imposition on her life and freedom. I came to love her over time, but that is getting ahead of the story. So, for now let me discuss more about my mother and my childhood.

At home, Mom oversaw the cooking, cleaning, and the rearing of the children as well as the running of the household while Dad worked to pay the bills. It was the 1960s, and President John F. Kennedy had just been shot. At that point, we were still a few years away from the moon landing.

Before I was born, my mom had been a teacher, but I never knew her in that role. I only knew her as Mom. She was a product of the times and was expected to give up her career to raise her children. She was ambitious and a feminist years before miniskirts and bra burnings. I believe she resented having to give up her career to stay home with the kids and her resentment was noticed by myself and my siblings. It appeared to be a lingering point of contention between my parents as well.

Mom was always concerned about how things would look and what people would think. Everything was always about her public image. Mom would always have a façade that everything was great. She was an attractive blonde woman who would go to the beauty parlor once a week to get her hair done. It was very important to her for her hair to be styled just right. She would readily engage others in conversation and was quick to smile or laugh if the other person had intelligence and a sense of humor. Mom enjoyed debating politics with those who had an opposing view.

My mother seemed to resent the family from holding her back. This was never spoken of, and she always felt nobody could tell if she was mad if she didn't rant and rave about something. But inside the household, we could read her emotions clearly. She had implosions rather than explosions. Her lips would tighten, she would hold her breath, and she would become extremely quiet as she sat cross-legged and had a cocktail while her foot spun in circles feverishly. We all knew she was having a repressed meltdown.

In many ways, my mom was probably a decade or so ahead of her time. She was vice chair of the Massachusetts Republican Party, a member of the City Council, a trustee to Worcester State College, and President of the Better Business Bureau of Worcester. Eventually, she ended up in Baltimore, Maryland judging multi-million-dollar arbitration claims. This allowed her prestige and got her away from the family as we all stayed behind in Massachusetts. I was far too young to appreciate her expertise and knowledge at that time and it was during this time that I landed in serious trouble.

The house that appeared perfect from the outside was a very different scenario inside. My parents both had drinking issues, but they drank in different ways. Dad was mostly never home, and when he was, he would usually pass out drunk in front of the TV after stopping off at the Lithuanian club before coming home from work. So, he was not often available to us. Mom, on the other hand, would start the day singing songs from popular musicals. As the day wore on, she would have highballs or cocktails, and her actions would become more unpredictable. She could become meaner and attack us verbally. I was never sure what highballs or cocktails were, but I knew that when my mom drank, she thought it leant her an air of sophistication and was therefore acceptable. She considered a drunk to be someone who was a gutter wino wearing a shabby coat and not a mother from the suburbs.

It is odd that as I look back on my early years now, I have no happy memories of my childhood with my mother. I can remember sterile facts like she was my Cub Scout den mother and that she had a nice smile. She would always worry about what kind of animals I would drag into the house - snakes, turtles, frogs, worms, birds, etc. But I don't have any emotional memories. I have no feeling of ever being wanted or of bonding with my mom. All that I do remember was feeling resented and unwanted. Eventually the problems with my mother would explode, but that was still years away.

I don't remember much dialogue between my parents except whether Dad wanted to buy a new car or truck versus putting that money toward house payments. They both believed you don't speak in front of the kids and kept their disputes behind closed doors.

Denise

My oldest sister Denise was born April 8, 1958 and was four years older than me. This did not lend itself well to bonding. In many ways, we were alike, or at least our paths would take similar routes. We came to be known as the "bad" kids while my brother Jon and sister Valerie became known as the "good" ones. I don't really know what qualifies as "bad kids" when you are nine and five years old, but this dynamic would play out all through our lives until her eventual death in 2018. We were never particularly close as kids due to that four-year difference, but I was always observing her and emulating her. As we grew older, this became more of an issue because she was always a willful and rambunctious girl. When she was in her early teens, she was already using drugs. I would watch her and her friends, and they seemed to be so cool. They were all products of the 1970s. The music was radical to reflect the times, the Vietnam War was on the TV every night, and protests were beginning to occur on campuses for civil rights, human rights, women's rights. Although the fall of Saigon was still years away, the tie-dyed shirts and bell bottom jeans were grabbing my attention in a big way.

I remember Denise mostly by two things: her music, and the fact that she could usually be counted on to have some sort of emotional or mental health crisis at Christmas when the family was getting together. Mom wanted the ideal Norman

Rockwell Christmas but that never seemed to materialize. Denise's music was the psychedelic style of the day. Jefferson Airplane, Cream, and the Stones, but she also liked Tower of Power, A Taste of Honey, and the Ohio Players. These interested me because I wasn't familiar with them.

Val

My sister Valerie was born October 10, 1960, and she is two years older than me. She is not my big sister; I am her little brother, which is our private joke because I am 6'4" and 265 lbs. I always envied her because life seemed easy for her. Even as kids she had the ability to effortlessly make friends. The teachers and grown-ups liked her because she was a well-behaved child. As far as the dynamic in our household went, Val and my brother Jon were considered the good ones, while Denise and I were the bad kids.

I know parents are supposed to love their kids equally, but that was not the case in our household. My sister Val did well in school and earned good grades. She was the helpful, considerate, responsible child while I was the screwup, got bad grades, and made no friends. These positive qualities of my sister would last a lifetime. She still has good friends, is still responsible, and is still helpful - all qualities that I would appreciate in the coming years.

My sister's only bad luck in childhood seemed to be that she was severely allergic to poison ivy and was prone to receiving bad haircuts. She had a shag and a perm that would blow up into a little blond afro on very humid days. Val was a bit of a tomboy, and we used to fight all the time until I learned that boys shouldn't be hitting girls, especially brothers and sisters. She enjoyed animals, the woods, the water, and motorcycles. Her passion for animals and motorcycles still exists. When we were going to school, I believe she just considered me a pain in the ass. But I looked up to her and liked talking to some of her friends because they seemed marginally accepting of me.

When we were kids, my sister Val had a pony named Marshmallow, a Morgan/Arabian horse named Bingo, and a Huskie named Argo over which she was very possessive. One day when my sister went to school, I saddled up Bingo and took him for a ride. I didn't know it at the time, but a local reporter saw me on the horse and put our picture in the paper with the caption "Mr. Sinnott and his horse Bingo were out riding." Wow! She was so furious at me not only for stealing the horse but for claiming it as my own that she never forgave me. So, to correct a historical inaccuracy, let me state for the record that I, Jeffrey Sinnott, did steal my sister's horse that day. The horse belonged to her and not to me. I wish to atone for that long-ago sin.

Val was both my rival and my friend. We would go and feed the animals at a nearby petting zoo that also had a couple of rides. The goats would charge us and knock us down, and the camels and llamas would spit at us. Also, the chickens would attack us. Somehow, surviving this ordeal together we came out as two kids who had just triumphed over life's toughest trials. (Oh, how innocent we were.)

I remember Denise and Val picking rhubarb stalks out of the shaded garden by the back door on Mower Street where the path led out to the grape arbor. We could pick fresh grapes from the vine that covered our barbeque area. They would grab handfuls of rhubarb and a bowl of sugar for dipping the stalks. Eating one stalk after another, not wanting to share them with me.

Jon

My brother Jon, the youngest, was born on April 5, 1965. He is three years younger than me, 4 inches shorter, and has my dad's hairline. He was my mom's favorite child and could do no wrong in her eyes. He and Val were my dad's favorites as well. I believe my brother looked up to me, and in hindsight I wish he had found someone else he could look up to because I set a bad example for him to follow.

I suppose that, like most older brothers, I picked on him more than I should have. But I also really liked him. He was open, trusting, and down for whatever I suggested. He even had a good sense of humor. Jon was a good kid, and I understood why my folks labeled him as such. I can't think of him without remembering swimming, fishing, canoeing, and exploring the woods, fields, and ponds around our house.

Jon and I would always bring critters into the house, and Mom was always yelling at us about not leaving hornpout (catfish) in the sink, not to leave turtles, newts, pollywogs, or other living creatures swimming around in the mud room sinks. She would tell us not to put Garter snakes that we harvested from the surrounding rock walls in any drawers. She damn near had a conniption fit, "Do not throw any more snakes into the tub when Denise is in there!" Seemed funny but caused a horrible fear of snakes for Denise.

My brother and I were always fishing, exploring, riding bikes, or exploring the woods and fields. Jon was ready to follow my lead anywhere, and usually his only question was "Can we bring the dogs?" We always had dogs and tried to take them everywhere. We could have an enjoyable day just digging for worms or digging for antique bottles at the old dump on the property at Mower Street.

We had many pets over the years, not counting all the stray animals we would pull in. I most remember the Irish setters. They are beautiful dogs and great for kids, but boy, are they stupid. They would forever be chasing cars and coming home from the woods with a face full of porcupine quills.

The other thing I was remembering was Jon and me finding a giant snapping turtle in the mill pond brook. We captured the turtle with the idea of bringing it home. Walking into the Finest Supermarket beside CVS and Friendly's, we asked for a bag or cart to carry the snapping turtle in, horrifying the clerks and customers. I don't think the turtle fit in the bag, as its claws were huge, but we grabbed a shopping cart and walked it home. We kept the thing all summer in deep sinks in the mud room (transitional room where you could take your muddy boots off). We eventually released it back into Mill Pond but not before it took a little piece of us with him back into the wild.

As I became a teen and never came home, Jon and I had less contact. I think he was very scared of and for me, because I was always getting into things I shouldn't be. This usually meant me stealing his savings or being a general nuisance.

As a child, I remember us living in three separate houses. The first was on Dawson Road near Cook's Pond and the local reservoirs. This was a dirt road surrounded by woods in the middle of a flood plain. We loved it. Mom, not so much. We stayed for a number of years and then moved 4 miles away to the second house on Wild Rose Avenue. We were told it was "a better neighborhood, with a swimming pool." Many kids on the street were envious and would come over during the summer months to go for a swim. I liked swimming at night when I could see the fireflies.

We again stayed for a few years and were told we were moving 1 mile away to Liberty Farm on Mower Street. This was a historical landmark built in the 1700's that used to be part of the Underground Railroad. An informal hodgepodge of houses and people that helped slaves escape from the South to freedom in the Northern States. In the 1700's this was the only house around for miles because it was all agricultural area. This house was still bigger than the surrounding houses and had fields, stone walls, gardens and trees to climb where we could run around and play.

The house was originally owned by Abbey Kelly Foster who was a famous abolitionist and women's rights advocate. The three addresses also meant that I was often transferring between schools. I attended six schools before dropping out in the tenth grade - Tatnuck, West Tatnuck, Chandler Junior High, Worcester Vocational Tech, and finally, Doherty High and South High.

School

I will speak of grammar school first and deal with high school later although some timelines may overlap. In most people's lives, grammar school is a time of relative ease. It is a time to play with other kids while learning to interact. In my case, grammar school represented a time of instability and early trauma in my life. I was always a bad student. Starting in kindergarten where I spoke with a lisp that required a speech therapist. Therapy lasted through the first grade. I believe that I was developmentally delayed or had some kind of learning disability, but back then, conditions like Oppositional Defiance Disorder and ADHD were not recognized. A lisp will not help a child fit in with his peers, and it left me ostracized from the other kids, and self-conscious. I was coming from a home where I didn't feel wanted, and my classmates' rejection just seemed to confirm that I couldn't fit in anywhere.

This feeling would be constantly reinforced because I was always the new kid in class and trying to find my place to fit in with others, knowing I never would. During the fourth and fifth grades, I needed a tutor because I was failing math and struggling with everything else. School was so overwhelming. I don't know how kids can be failing in those grades, but it must be due to not meeting learning objectives for those age groups.

The one lesson learned while being shuffled between schools was that I had to fight the local bully. If I didn't, the problems would only get worse. Win or lose, I at least established my place in the pecking order. I had few friendships in school or with kids from the neighborhood. I knew as I thought about entering junior high that things were going to get a whole lot worse. I just didn't know how bad it would turn out to be.

Chapter 2
Losing My Way

Nature v. nurture?

Negative messaging v. positive messaging?

Sibling rivalry v. emotional abuse?

As an adult, I have reflected on the messaging that my sister Denise and I received: "You're bad, you're stupid, you're lazy, you're unsociable and unlikable, you can't do anything right, and everything is your fault."

Contrast that with the messaging that my sister Val and brother Jon received: "You're smart, you're likeable, it's not your fault, and you can do anything you put your mind to."

I wonder if it is really a surprise that these groups of siblings experienced such wildly different outcomes? My sister Denise and I (the bad ones) ended up as alcoholic drug addicts with felony convictions while Val and Jon (the good ones) ended up being responsible and having successful 30-plus-year careers in nursing.

Most people don't have turning points in their lives at ten years old, but I did. Although I estimate that I was ten years old, it could have been anywhere from 10 to 12, and the periods likely overlap. Critical things happened when I turned ten years old. I started smoking, drinking, and using drugs, and my mother decided to rejoin the workforce. Not only did she return to work, but she also decided to go into politics. Not only did she go into politics, but she went into politics as a Republican in the Democratic stronghold of Massachusetts (yikes!). She decided to run for City Council, and all of us kids were horrified, none of us wanted her to seek public office. Once all of her political signs went up around town, kids started treating me differently. Instead of just being "Jeff", I took on the moniker of "the politician' s kid." I was never popular anyway, and now I knew I was in the crosshairs of every local bully. Mom lost the election the first time out, but instead of quitting, she decided to run again. We all hated her politician friends and their phony smiles. We hated that Mom would roll us out in front of the press as props for her campaign to make her look like a doting mother. We hated when she would host cocktail parties or fundraisers at the house because it meant that she would ignore us all night.

One night, she hosted a fundraiser, and I was trying to get her attention, but she kept ignoring me. I couldn't tell the reader what I needed, but I can tell you that I got frustrated when she ignored me. I tried repeatedly to get her attention. I began to have an emotional meltdown, and she tried to quiet me down. I told her, "I hate you - you don't even care about me, all you care about is your stupid political friends. You don't love me!"

She turned around and hissed at me, "You little shit, I wish you were never born!" That one statement validated everything I had felt in the house for years. I knew that I was unwanted, resented, and a burden to her. At that point I shut down emotionally. I no longer wanted to live under their roof where I was unwanted. I would do everything possible to get out of that house.

I deeply internalized that statement "I wish you were never born," and that thought drove my actions for years to come.

At ten years old, I didn't yet have the means to live in the world, but I could escape into drugs and alcohol. I began to tap into the liquor cabinet at home. Those indulgences allowed me to at least bury the rage that I felt inside. The problem was that I preferred being lost in oblivion more than focusing on the anger and pain I was feeling. At ten or eleven, I lacked the knowledge to speak to what was going on inside me. I felt that God hated me, that the world was against me, that I shouldn't have been born, and that I was doomed to suffer. This was my attitude as I headed off to junior high school, where bigger bullies, more cliques, and harder drugs awaited me.

Junior high went as expected. There were fights, and I was bullied. I found connections, got suspended, and received lousy grades. I began drinking increasingly as it was the only way I felt accepted. Although I fit in with the stoners at school, I was already much more committed to getting drunk and stoned than they were. They got high to socialize while I got drunk and high to feed the craving and to cope. I used acid, valium, meth, morphine, pot, mushrooms, dilaudid, and anything else I could get my hands on. Because I was using more than other kids,

I got to know more of the local drug dealers. I met criminal elements from various parts of the city. As my teen years went on, I was able to find people who would buy the things I stole to feed my habit. My life kept getting more complicated and riskier.

The principal at Chandler Junior High was an older balding black man named Johnny Law (yes, that really was his name), and he had been terrifying kids at that school forever. When I enrolled, he approached me and asked if Denise was my sister, to which I admitted she was.

"Aha, I see, I am going to have to keep an eye on you, Mr. Sin-nott, and in fact, I am going to make you my project."

That brief exchange set the stage for the next year. After suffering through one year of junior high with Johnny Law, I decided the next year to instead head off to boys' trade, Worcester Regional Vocational Technical School, where I would last for one year in the machine shop learning how to run a lathe and mill. I was suspended from this school for fighting again. This fight would almost cost me my arm because when I punched a kid in the mouth, I got cellulitis (a bacterial infection that spread rapidly). The next day at school I passed out cold in class because my whole right arm ballooned up with infection and needed to be transported to the hospital where I spent almost a full month. That was the end of trade school.

Each year I would have to attend summer school because I was always in danger of failing. This was the place where all the other delinquents, druggies, and criminals were forced into intensive classes together. The teachers passed us each year because they didn't want to be responsible for holding us back and because it would be a bad reflection on them if they did. If they couldn't get "D" students to pass, it spoke to their ability to teach.

I knew I would never be accepted as the person I was, but by embracing the labels of 'rebel' and 'loner' it seemed to provide me cover. With these labels I knew what people were expecting of me. I had become more anti-social anyway. I would reject people before they could reject me. I knew that people would never love me, but I could make them hate me. Attention for negativity is better than no attention. Yes, it was a dysfunctional way of looking at the world, but at that point in my life it was empowering, even if in a negative way.

The next two years found me attending both South High and Doherty Memorial High School. I could not relate to any of the students in my classes. Eventually, I just gave up the pretext of trying to learn. When I had questions, the teachers never wanted to explain something and acted as if I were supposed to know it intuitively. I don't know exactly why I struggled in school, but I seemed unable to grasp the concepts from kindergarten on up.

My only friend during my teen years was someone I will call George (not his real name). We met when I was around twelve, and he lived with his grandmother a couple of miles away. He was the only person who accepted me as I was. He didn't have a problem with my having a mom who was a politician. George didn't have many friends, either. We talked about our dysfunctional families, and we came from different places in life, but the commonality was our messy households. He grew up in the projects with a background of poverty, and his mother's boyfriend was abusive to him. George never really went to school, either, except to attend an alternative school for a year before dropping out completely.

Two kids without much to do and time on their hands can find mischief to get into. Many days we would get stoned and hang out downtown. During our days we would come across other kids doing the same thing. Sometimes, we would befriend them, but other times we would buy drugs from them or sell drugs to them. Every now and then, a fight would break out, and we might end up fighting, robbing, or ripping them off. We never had any kind of plan as to how our days would turn out, we would wait and see what happened.

George and I were always drinking, which was the primary bond between us. As we got further away from our early teens, we became more mobile and ventured out more. I had a small green Honda CB360 and could use my folks' car regularly. George had a couple of cars at different points, too. Sometimes I wouldn't have a vehicle and would stay out all night stealing whatever we could find to sell. I would break into places, rob people, or buy and sell drugs depending on whatever opportunity presented itself. I would hook up with single moms on welfare and stay with them from time to time. I kept clothes at various locations around the city. Depending on who I was cool with at any given time would determine where I stayed.

Sometimes I would be out all night, prowling the streets like a wolf or hyena and looking to victimize whoever I could, feeding on the bones of society. Occasionally this would work out, and I would wake up with wads of money. Other times, I would come to with my head kicked in, covered in blood, with my entire body looking and feeling like I had been beaten with a sledgehammer. I was a raging alcoholic and didn't know how NOT to drink. Teenagers are often rash, impulsive, and make bad decisions. I was more stubborn than most and unwilling to quit. I was never a master criminal making big scores, nor was I a major drug dealer selling volumes of drugs. Instead, I was just a knuckleheaded kid trying to stay ahead of a bad drinking problem. Even now, after almost forty years, I can remember the feeling of having been up all night, never making it home, being completely hung over, and wishing I could die. I would make it to AA (Alcoholics Anonymous) several times at others' insistence but was too young to admit defeat.

George and I would always be out after the bars closed. At that time of night, only the drunks, druggies, police officers, and madmen are out. We thrived in this environment. People from all over the city would run into each other at the Store 24s, the Seven-Elevens, the AM/ PM, and the minimarts. The names of these places change in different cities, but they are the places where you can buy cigarettes, a microwavable burrito, rolling papers, and munchies at three AM. I knew this had to stop, as I was getting arrested for more charges and increasingly more serious offenses. My DUIs were becoming assaults, robberies, assaults with dangerous weapons, and so on. I hated myself and everyone else.

I had no positive people in my life, or at least could not see them at the time, and felt like I didn't deserve any positivity. The world was shit.

At seventeen, the court gave me the option of joining the military instead of going to jail. I leapt at the chance. I figured if I was going to do something, I should do it all the way, so I joined the Marines (Marine Reserves). I went to boot camp at Parris Island and then went to communication school to be a radio operator/wireman. I was never a gung-ho Marine, but I was away from home and still able to drink and get high. Even in the Marines I could not get away from myself, and my problems continued from my own behavior.

One night I was supposed to be doing fire watch duty in the barracks, but I passed out drunk with a lit cigarette and damn near burned the barracks down with everyone sleeping. I would eventually complete training and make my way back to Worcester, which is where my reserve unit was located. I did all right for a while because we were only required to train one weekend a month and serve two weeks a year while training. But then I couldn't even do that right. Every time our unit was scheduled for training, I ended up in jail. The Marines soon got tired of this and bounced me out of the military with a general discharge for frequent involvement with civilian authorities.

Once, while I was in the in 'house of correction', I ended up earning my GED (General Equivalency Diploma), which turned out to be one of the best things in my life, as it would eventually allow me to enroll in college and take classes.

The last of my teen years found me living in Los Angeles where I had moved to get away from Worcester and all the negative influences. I had heard from my mother that my cousin had been sober in AA for years. I contacted him, and he initially gave me a place to live. I found work which allowed me to buy a truck. Then I used it to do light deliveries around town. I would manage to stay sober in AA for a year. I got a small apartment, liked the girls in L. A., and started to feel good about myself. This should have been a warning sign. I started seeing a married/separated woman which quickly became very complicated. Her husband and his family were very wealthy with some dirty money. He didn't seem to acknowledge that they were separated. He bought her a brand-new truck to try to win her back. Two weeks later, I was seen driving it up in the canyons about one in the morning and was run off the road by one of her husband's employees. A couple weeks after that my truck was strafed by bullets while stopped at a red light. My world was beginning to unravel, and I was beginning to drift away from the A.A. people. I would leave the girl, leave A.A and ended up in a serious altercation with a young gang kid. I would lose my job, and my life fell apart. I decided to leave Los Angeles and headed back to Worcester.

Fairly quickly, I relapsed and returned to the darkness of my unhealthy habits. There is a reason that AA people tell you not to get involved with other AA people for at least a year. That is because people coming to rehab usually have unwise decision-making skills when they come into the program.

At 21 years old, I was back in Worcester doing odd jobs to make beer money. George was in Worcester and now married - or at least trying to be. He and I still drank, but he had new friends at that time. He was working with a couple guys that I didn't know well. I knew Dana a little bit but had just met Dave over the previous month. I had been trying to stay sober and attended AA meetings. Then I enrolled in the local community college and took a full-time job that was supposed to start the following week. Finally, it felt like I was on the right track.

That week I had worked with George and told him about my good fortune. He was happy for me. We decided to go out to celebrate because we didn't know when we would be able to get together again. We met up at George's house early that evening and made plans for the night. Someone had said there were bands playing at a couple of the clubs and that they were supposed to have happy hour specials. After sitting around drinking some beers, we decided to go to a bar in Leicester, Massachusetts. I had been there one other time but was not a regular. We stayed from 8:00 to 11:00, and I had maybe a dozen White Russians and a handful of beers.

At around 11:00 or 11:30, we decided to head out to another bar before closing time. This bar in a nearby town also had a band and drink specials, so we headed to Oxford and paid the admission to get in. I went up front by the stage to listen to the band while George and Dave headed off in search of drugs.

A half hour later they returned with a couple of guys and said they were going out to the parking lot. I didn't know anyone in the bar, so I followed them. When we got to Allen Tate's car, he said he didn't want that many people in the vehicle, so I said I would wait in Dave's car and for them to get me when they were done. I laid down on the big bench seat that all cars had back in those days and waited for them to return with drugs.

After a few minutes I heard arguing in the parking lot and looked up to see what was going on. George and Allen were arguing about the quality of cocaine that George had bought. George thought the coke he got as a "sampler" was not the same as what they bought. I exited the car and saw George and Allen face off. John Peters, who was Allen's friend, was standing behind him as though to provide additional muscle. I stood behind George to balance the odds.

George swung quickly at Allen, and Allen attempted to swing back. It was on, like so many times before. I ran past George, kicking Allen on my way, and swung immediately at John Peters. George and Allen looked like they were locked in battle and heading to the ground. I engaged John, and after we exchanged punches, John charged my middle as though grabbing me in a bear hug. I hit him in the head and ribs, which didn't make him disengage, so I kneed him in the face. He broke off and walked backwards to the bar to get reinforcements.

As John headed into the bar for help, I looked at George who was on top of Allen. George was trying to elbow Allen in the face. Allen was grabbing George's arm to stop him, and I told George,

"Let's get out of here before he comes back with friends."

George stood up, panting, trying to catch his breath, huffing and puffing. I looked back once more to make sure no one was coming yet and saw Allen at my knee beginning to get up. If he stood, it would slow our escape, and we would be hugely outnumbered. Without thinking, I spontaneously kicked Allen in the face. He fell over backward, and George and I put the boots to him as we did, the anticipated help poured out the bar's back door into the parking lot, and we fled the scene with people yelling and screaming at us.

I stayed on the George's couch that night. The next morning, we found out Allen was dead. Dave came over the next morning and said he saw it on the news. I didn't want to believe it. Later, the reality and magnitude of what had happened hit me. I knew that my life was going to change. I would be going to prison. No amount of wishing otherwise would change that.

Allen's death was unintended, we didn't go to the bar with the intent of killing anyone. There were no weapons involved except feet, and it was only through chance that we even met those guys. But with the witnesses in the parking lot there was NO chance that we were not going to be arrested. I spent a couple of days drinking and wishing it hadn't happened... but there was no going back.

A couple of days later, I was arrested at my folks' house by the State Police. I gave a statement mostly denying blame and throwing responsibility on George. When George was arrested, he denied responsibility as well and threw the weight on me. At that point in our lives, at that age, neither of us was willing to accept responsibility. I would have been willing to plead guilty to second degree to save my ass at the time, but I didn't know it was an option.

It is no surprise that this was the action of two young men dealing with such circumstances. I knew immediately that we were in deep trouble. There were numerous witnesses, our statements were used against us, neither of our lawyers presented a defense, and the court tried us together rather than separately. Neither one of us took the stand. It was only six months from arrest to conviction, and my lawyer only visited twice for about a half hour each time.

My lawyer tried to enter a plea bargain of manslaughter but never told me that I could plead guilty to second degree murder. He never explained the difference between first and second-degree murder or the concept of extreme atrocity or cruelty that would support the first-degree murder conviction. When he did finally explain this to me, it was two weeks into the trial, and he asked if I was willing to plead guilty. I told him,

"Yes, go make that happen."

He came back ten minutes later and said it was too late because we were two weeks into the trial. It seems to me that my lawyer should have explained this to me far earlier.

In looking back on my life and trying to figure out why things happened the way they did. I need to revisit those early years. Why was I bullied? Why is anyone bullied?

I was bullied because kids are mean, because I spoke with a lisp, and because I was always the new kid. I was bullied because I was not popular. I was isolated and alone. I was bullied because I was timid and lacked confidence and self-worth and did not know how to navigate social circles. I was bullied because I saw myself as the victim, my mother didn't want me, God didn't want me, and society didn't want me. That began to change as I became the antisocial rebel loner. I would no longer be a victim. I would hurt others before they could hurt me and victimize others before they could victimize me. This justified my actions of lashing out at the world.

As a grownup who has done his own childhood trauma work, I can say that I took on the labels and façades of antisocial rebel loner as a means of protection. Accepting these labels empowered me to act out negatively. It no longer mattered how immoral I acted, who I hurt, or the consequences of my actions. If they didn't care about me, why should I care about anyone else?

As a teen, those labels were a defense mechanism. As an adult, I recognize the impact the labels and traumas had on my life. I no longer live in victimhood. As an adult, I am in charge of my actions and the consequences of those actions. I no longer blame others for my misfortunes, and I can see my damaged inner child with compassion, empathy, understanding, and forgiveness.

This is why I facilitate prison programs today. Having walked through life on a path of darkness and emerging on a path of light, I am in a unique position to help others deal with their traumas, manage the ways in which they try to cope with them, and help them escape lives of crime and addiction. I try to steer them in the direction of personal responsibility, ownership of their actions, and acting with moral integrity. I hope the men who get out of prison never return, and instead, go on to live successful lives in society without being a threat to themselves or others as they return to their communities.

Chapter 3

Prison: The Early Years

I believe my mental and emotional growth were stunted as a teen due to the trauma with my mother as well as my addictions to alcohol and drugs starting so early in life. Frequently moving from place to place and having to acclimate to new people and new environments was detrimental to me.

Going to prison is likewise a traumatic experience to anyone who has never been there. That was certainly true in my case. I would say that when I came to prison at age 22, I had been arrested at age 21 and convicted at 22. I was operating at the emotional maturity of a typical 12-year-old. My reasoning and problem-solving abilities were grossly delayed as well. Because of this I struggled when entering the prison system.

Abandon all hope ye who enter here.

—Dante Alighieri

Nothing can prepare a person for the experience of entering a maximum-security prison. This is especially true when you have just been sentenced to a first-degree life sentence. (This means a life sentence without parole.) Life without parole is a very slow death sentence. No matter how whitewashed the exterior prison walls may be, the inside walls are dark places where monsters lurk, waiting to steal your soul, figuratively, if not literally.

Upon my arrival at Walpole State Prison, I was escorted in shackles and handcuffs still wearing my suit from court to the inside lobby and into the control booth. When you are taken somewhere in cuffs and shackles, it is a sure sign that your life has not turned out as planned. The county guards handed my paperwork through the metal slot to the state guards in the booth., and the state guards came out to take possession of me.

The guards said, "Okay, let's go," and indicated that I should head in the direction of a thick metal door on the far side of the metal detector. As we approached the door, it started to open on its own since a guard was controlling it from inside the booth. As the door opened, I could see into the little room beyond and saw another metal door beyond. We entered the "trap" area, and the first door closed behind us. The door in front of us opened only after the rear door loudly locked. I knew at that moment and with each subsequent door, I was leaving everyone and everything I knew behind. After going through two more doors, we entered the interior of the infamous Walpole State Prison.

1 was under escort as the metal door aggressively closed behind me. I paused for just a second and looked around. Behind and above me was the main control tower, seemingly 100 feet above my head. I looked off to the left and saw whitewashed walls along with a guard tower in the distance. I looked right and saw the same thing on the other side. We were in what is known as the "dead zone," which is the area between the last fence and the wall. If an inmate were in here unescorted, he would be considered trying to escape. It felt like a nightmare, but I was wide awake.

As we began to walk, I could feel a pall of tension and negativity hanging over the entire place. We headed left toward what I would learn was the hospital and new inmate section. The hospital is upstairs, and the "new man" section is downstairs. The new man section is where new prisoners are processed into the prison and where the degradation really begins.

First, the guards strip you. As your clothes hit the floor, you realize that you are no longer in control of your life. You may not know it at that point, but you will be getting naked for the guards for the rest of your sentence.

You recognize that the situation is serious and that no one can help you now. Instead of being a person at liberty in society, you have become a thing, an object, a noun. You have become a commodity to be controlled and regulated, the guards and staff stress this point to you immediately. Prison is a huge reality check. As you try and get your wits about you, it becomes painfully apparent that the world you knew no longer exists.

The next question that pops into your mind is how will you adapt to your new environment? Some convicts entering prison already knowing former acquaintances who are serving time there. They have a huge jump on finding their way because they have alliances from their cities, towns, projects, gangs, and other associations.

Forty years ago, I would say most white Americans didn't know someone in prison. That was certainly true in my case. Forty years later, many families have a loved one doing time, whether that is a father, uncle, brother, son, or nephew as well as female relatives and friends, too.

New inmates without someone to guide them have a difficult path ahead. There are many perils and ways to crash out (run into problems). When you enter the system, if a new guy doesn't know anyone, he is usually asked, "Where are you from? Who do you know? What are you in for?" The inmates will try to point him in the direction of residents from his area, but that is no guarantee that he will be accepted by them. Finding a place where you fit in is important because you are being judged by every person in the prison from the cons to the guards, and they are assessing you harshly. Prison is a predatory place, and many prisoners are masters of manipulation. It is easy for a new guy to get caught up in things and to become a "crash dummy." A crash dummy is a person who is manipulated by others to go on a mission that usually entails stabbing a rival. Guys are told, "If you do as we say, we will like you, accept you, and have your back." The implication is that if you do not do it, you will become their enemy.

Sometimes inmates will pull a guy into their circle, but usually it is only if they expect to have problems in the future. People who are crash dummies are always expendable. They become pawns on the prison chessboard.

When you enter the prison, it seems like everything is going a million miles an hour and that everyone knows everyone else except you. Hopefully, a new arrival begins to find his way around and fit in somewhere. Prisons, especially maximum-security facilities, are inherently violent and dangerous places. There are countless ways of getting into trouble without even knowing it.

As time goes on, things begin to slow down, and you see who is who and what is what. You learn that every chow table is segregated first by race, then by area, then by streets, projects, and gangs. You may begin to work if you are so inclined. This can kill time, keep you out of harm's way, and even put a couple of dollars in your canteen account. Jobs typically pay $1 per hour, which is another sign that you have left the real world.

One of the first jobs I took in Walpole was working in the library and the law library, which were both in the same area. This allowed me to learn about law, work on my case, and stay busy. I learned how to sue the Department of Correction over minor property issues and even won a couple cases. This made me feel good, and I was able to be of limited help to other prisoners. The guards, however, always hate inmates they consider trying to be "legal beagles." I was never that good at law, but the guards saw what they wanted to see.

I had been working in the law library for six months when my mom came up for a visit. She asked what I was doing and how it was going. I told her that the law library was fairly good, but the general library was limited and lacked books. I never gave this another thought until a month or so later when my mom came up for another visit. She told me that she had been in touch with her friend, Senator Arthur Chase. Senator Chase called the prison and offered to donate an entire library for free. The prison warden at the time declined the offer and reportedly said, "Why would I want to give them a better library? They are so much easier to control when they are stupid and ignorant." Instead of wanting to educate and rehabilitate us, they were working actively against us.

This would become more of an issue later when we heard rumors that we were going to be eligible to receive Pell grants and take college courses.

I wanted to take college classes. I also knew that if college courses became available, the administration and the guards were going to be resentful and would become an impediment to our graduating. I was now glad that I had received my General Equivalency Degree while in the house of correction. I had no reason to think that I could even manage college classes based on how I had performed in high school. What I did know was that I had never done anything that could be considered an accomplishment in life, and I wanted to try.

I ended up going to Ten Block (Walpole's segregation unit at the time) many times for disruptive and assaultive conduct. This is the section of Walpole where some of the state's most violent and dangerous rapists and murderers are kept - the worst of the worst. The phrasing "worst of the worst" and "the state's most violent and dangerous rapist murderers" was the general statement to the *Boston Globe* and the *Boston Herald* from the Department of Corrections (D.O.C.)'s press releases in reference to us.

The max end of Walpole consisted of eight blocks of 45 men in each block. There were 15 cells on a tier. Each cell had bars on the front and looked out on a concrete wall. Toward the top of the wall was an enclosed catwalk leading to a centrally located control booth where the guards could monitor the block and open and close the cell doors.

The roofs were constructed of a plastic that let the outside light filter in.

Each block had a giant circulation fan that was deafening, but over time you got used to it. It was worse when the fan shut off because every sound echoed off the walls. This usually consisted of yelling, arguments, slamming dominos on the metal tables, disputes about dominoes, and the blaring of NWA and Public Enemy on the radios (which I hated). Sometimes, Jody Whatley and C+C music factory would be playing, and I could at least tolerate that. The minimum end of the prison consisted of 72 cells with solid doors and windows. The cells were arranged in an oval on three tiers, and on the top tier there was a railing that went all the way around the oval so you could look down on the first and second floors.

Above the third floor was a high roof with glass windows where snipers could be positioned to fire into the block with tear gas or lead if needed. The guards were stationed at a desk. When they wanted to open and close cells, they had to enter a control booth on the second floor, which was accessible by key. There were three blocks in the minimum end. Each block had a day room with card tables, a ping pong table, and a pool table. Ten Block, the segregation unit, was located by itself. It consisted of two stories and four tiers, two on the left and two on the right. Each cell had both bars on the doors and a solid door beyond that, which was locked by a guard from outside the door. In the summer, guards tended to lock you in your cell with the heat blasting. In the winter, guards would open all the windows on the tier and shut the heat off half the time. I remember being locked in my cage many nights with power off, so I would be forced to read by what little sliver of light filtered through the bottom of the door.

The colors in prisons are usually psychologically based, Battleship gray for anonymity and to erase any individuality. Red was used on gang units. Aggressive. Warlike. I was frequently in the hole for assaults on the guards, they tended to take it personally. I was locked in for my defiance, so I had it coming, but thank God I eventually found a better way of dealing with them and with my authority issues.

I can tell you that men on Ten Block with me at the time had good qualities. They were bright, intelligent, encouraging, and thoughtful. We were enthusiastic about college courses coming into the prison. Everyone acknowledged that they had run afoul of the law, like me, but they also said they wanted to try and be successful at something. There were reasons that many of these men came to prison aside from their crimes: alcohol abuse, drug addiction, poverty, racism, mental health, sexual and physical abuse in childhood.

Although not the direct cause of their crimes, these circumstances most certainly contributed to their life outcomes.

We discussed how the D.O.C. and the press label us stereotypically. Each of us felt degraded, debased, and demeaned. We all wanted to prove that we could be better than they described us. We laughed about what they would say when we graduated college. The D.O.C. would have to eat their words! We were not talking idly. Each and every man on the tier with me would eventually graduate. Not a single one ever came back to prison! I had always been defiant, but graduating college and proving to the D.O.C., the world, society, and myself that I was not a savage or an animal was a new positive, goal-directed defiance that I could live with.

The press' description of us as the "worst of the worst" and the "State's most violent and dangerous" has been around a long time. That characterization is still used to humiliate and degrade us in that manner when the politicians want to portray us a savages and animals that need to be controlled and they want to appear "tough on crime."

I would like to write a different narrative. I have chosen how I want to write this book. I decided if I was going to write a prison book, it couldn't be talking about murders, rapes, stabbings, gang conflicts, or fighting the system. It needed to be about the struggles of one man trying to come to grips with his past. The book had to be about how I have navigated the obstacles on my path and the way by which I have come to a different place in my life. I hope it can help someone else in their journey.

I want readers to consider points of view that may challenge his or her perspectives. I want the readers to ask themselves what they would do. How would they handle the situation? How would they find meaning to life?

Because I have dealt with the skeletons in my closet, I am in the unique position of being able to speak about my failures and achievements without having to worry about people's judgments. I own my faults rather than hide them. I hope you can be intrigued and find meaning along the way. I wrote the narrative in this book, but I ask you to consider all the Ten Block men that graduated. The line between freedom and captivity is thin and can happen to anyone in an instant from one wrong decision.

Every one of these men were written off by society, yet their determination to become better men would win in the end. These men had hopes and dreams of self-improvement and becoming better citizens, fathers, brothers, uncles, and sons.

I have been in the world long enough to know that education is one of the keys to success. Whether you define success as getting out of prison, earning sufficient income to support a family, or escaping degrading circumstances, education is key. In our coursework, the professors had no problem believing in us, but the powers that be wanted to see us fail. One group was trying to lift us up while the other was trying to keep us down.

When I enrolled in college, I was absolutely flabbergasted when the instructors said, "Read this and tell me what you think of it." You want to know what I think? Really? I could not believe that they not only were interested in my thoughts, but they also wanted me to expound on and defend my views as well. This was unexpected.

As I began to read and learn, I also realized just how ignorant I was of so many things in life. I became a knowledge-hungry sponge, wanting to learn about all subjects under the sun. When I had enough credits to choose my major, I chose psychology because I wanted answers as to what had gone wrong in my life.

I am closer to those answers now than when I graduated, but that is because I have never stopped looking for information and asking the necessary questions.

In 1988, I received an associate degree in Liberal Arts and General Studies from Bunker Hill Community College. In 1990, I earned a bachelor's degree from Curry College with a major in Psychology. I was Valedictorian of my small class and thanked all the professors who had been willing to give their time and effort helping those who society had written off. I knew the guards would often hassle the instructors on their way into the institution, but the professors were able to carry themselves with grace under pressure despite the obstacles they faced.

To someone who spent his teen years pickled on drugs and alcohol, this was a major accomplishment. It was as though I had just come out of a fog, and my head was beginning to get clear. I suppose in a sense that is exactly what happened. My mind was cleansed from an alcohol-induced haze, and I started to mature.

As the 1980's were ending, two fairly significant things happened. First, a prisoner approached my cell very timidly and asked if he could speak to me. "sure" I said, "Come on in." He told me he received a letter from his son, and he asked if I could read it to him. He was very ashamed about not being able to read so I said "sure, okay." I read him the letter and he went on his way. About a week later we spoke again and this time I asked him about his son and his inability to read. He said that when he was in school there was a ton of violence in the home, and he couldn't sleep or concentrate in school and that he got frustrated and quit. He said he was embarrassed that he couldn't read, and he wanted to learn to read and write so that his son could be proud of him. I told him that if he was willing, I could teach him to read and write and he immediately agreed.

I had no experience teaching, but I instinctively knew what to do. We began working together twice a week and walking through the alphabet, the vowel and consonant sounds and the ai, ea, oo, combinations. Pretty soon we were doing small sentences. He worked hard and we did the exercises in my cell so he wouldn't be embarrassed in front of people. Before long we were working on the preterit and imperfect verbs as well as the gerunds. At the time I didn't know the names of these things, but I was able to describe them to him. He was able to grasp the concept of a one-time action that was over and done with vs. an action that was started in the past and continued to evolve. I knew how to teach even if I didn't know the language of teaching at that time. I just felt like I was trying to help him out at the time and had no idea that I would be setting the stage for myself as a teacher in the years to come.

The second significant thing to happen was that on July 12th, 1989, at 9:55 pm. I smoked my last cigarette. This was big for me because I had smoked a pack a day for ten years and when I quit it meant that I could be in charge of me. That I had at least a modicum of power in my own life, and that I could make a beneficial change in my life.

Please don't think that just because I took college courses, all was well in the world. I was still immature, defiant, rebellious, and obnoxious. I was still young. I would fall into depression because I was starting a life sentence and saw no hope in the future.

I went back to the hole repeatedly. While I was there, I would read. I don't know what I was expecting would happen when I became confrontational with the guards, but it usually resulted in getting my head busted and my ribs smashed.

It was about to turn 1990, and that was a bad time to be in prison.

Chapter 4

Personal and Family Changes

The imposition of a life sentence forced me to change every relationship in my life. My new circumstances affected every area of my life.

The first relationship that changed was my relationship with alcohol. When I had been on the streets, I tried many times to get sober but could never quite make it. I certainly knew the grip that alcohol had on me and admitted to myself that I was an alcoholic. But wanting to stop drinking and being able to stop were two different things. I simply didn't know how not to drink, couldn't fathom it. Watching friends dealing with heroin addictions allowed me to see what it looked like and helped me to understand my addiction. Heroin addiction made no sense to me because I never had a craving for the drug. My mind and body craved alcohol. I could not drink without drinking excessively. When I did, my problems always got worse.

I have attended AA in prison because I know that I am an alcoholic, but a funny thing happened when I came through the prison doors. It seemed as though God removed the desire to drink from me. I could only describe it as His grace or divine intervention that extinguished the desire because I have not found the need or desire to take a drink since I came to prison. My relationship with alcohol changed because now I viewed it as the enemy. It was my addiction to alcohol that ruined my life. I do not want the reader to think that I am blaming my alcohol addiction to shift the blame. I am responsible for my actions, but I do know that alcoholism was one of the contributing factors in my downfall. After I began to get sober and more clear-headed in prison, I knew I didn't want to drink or be around drunk people anymore.

To anyone who thinks there is no alcohol in prison, you are sadly mistaken. The men in prison get drunk all the time and usually act like complete idiots. My aversion to alcohol would show up almost immediately as people would ask me to drink with them.

"I'm all set with that," I would reply. I never wanted to be rude or appear judgmental when declining alcohol, but I never wanted to partake, either. When I was newly imprisoned, it became apparent that I was better off locking in early for the night (asking the guard to close my cell) if everyone was going to be getting smashed. I can't say that every time guys got drunk, bad things happened, but the potential certainly escalated. People would usually start out cheerful and smiling, but in the hours that followed, you could feel the mood shift and become darker. Sometimes all the drunken knuckleheads would end up fighting among themselves. Other times knives would come out, and people would get hurt, or a major brawl would break out because some drunken fool was spouting off, and everyone would get involved.

I remember calling home at Christmas and getting passed around on the phone to everyone - and getting a drunken ex-friend or acquaintance slobbering all over the receiver.

"How ya' been? I always loved ya', man. I always wanted to come see you, but the battery / tire / alternator / window…." – something was always broken. It was so ugly hearing people talk when they were drunk. I began to understand why friends and family had despised me when I was drunk. It doesn't matter if people tell you that they had good intentions to visit. Good intentions are only intentions until you act on them.

This is one of the lessons you learn when you first enter permanent detention. People either do what they say they are going to do – or don't. If they can't be counted on, then maybe you want to cast them out of your life (especially if you are serving a life sentence). This was one of the tenets of yoga that I would incorporate years later. Intentions without action count for nothing.

I identify as an alcoholic and an addict. The reason I put them in that order is because drinking came first. I would use every drug under the sun, but for me they were secondary. Drugs were used to fill the emotional void, but I never craved them the way I did alcohol. When I drank, it seemed to alter my brain chemistry. From the time I was ten or eleven years old, I was drunk until I turned twenty-one. I can't completely speak to what alcohol does to the adolescent mind, but I've heard it retards function in the developing brain. Therefore, I believe that emotionally when I came to prison, I was operating at the maturity level of a twelve-year-old.

On January 15, 2021, an article titled "Alcohol harms the brain in teen years – before and after that, too" was authored by Claire McCarthy, MD, a senior faculty editor at Harvard Health Publishing with the following insight to the effects of alcohol on the teenage mind.

In a recent editorial in *The BMJ*, a trio of scientists pointed out that there are three periods in life when the brain goes through major changes and is particularly vulnerable to the effects of alcohol.

One of those being years of transition between childhood and adulthood, the brain grows and changes in many important ways that are crucial for that transition to be successful. When teens and young adults drink alcohol, it can interfere with that process of brain development in ways that affect the rest of their lives. (Alcohol harms the brain in teen years — before and after that, too – Harvard Health)

Fortunately, I was miraculously freed of my desire to drink when incarcerated. But I don't want the reader to think that I was miraculously healed or cured of addiction.

I will always be an alcoholic (whether that desire to drink is evident or not), and I have always had addiction issues. When I first came to prison, the drugs available were heroin, valium, tuinol and dilaudid. The nature of drugs in prison changed over the years, and those drugs are now virtually nonexistent. K-2 and sobos (suboxone) would later come to dominate the prison landscape as they are so cheap.

My relationships with people were also changing. None would be more vital or difficult than with my mother. She came up to visit every weekend, and at first, I couldn't figure out why. We had never been one of those close-knit, lovey-dovey, touchy-feely families, and after being estranged from my folks all through my teen years, I could only surmise that she felt guilty.

I assured her that I was serving time because of my own doing, and it wasn't her fault. I reminded Mom that she had taught me morals and values, although they were deeply hidden, and there was little else she could have done. I would not have listened anyway. My mother was such a vain and narcissistic person that she was probably only concerned about how my being in prison would reflect on her parenting.

Whatever the reason for my mom's visits initially, I can only tell you that I am glad she did. I may not have appreciated her when I was a child, but each year that I was in prison, I valued her more. In the ensuing years, she would show me the value of family in ways that I couldn't have imagined, which was ironic given that family was what I had originally rebelled against. The family did come up to visit routinely, whether that was Mom, Dad, Denise, Val, or Jon. I never had good friendships or strong bonds on the street, so I wasn't surprised when few others missed me. I did have slightly better relationships with women than with men, and a few women visited me over the years although they have long since disappeared. My relationships with men were contentious and challenging, so I would need to work on those in time.

What I saw immediately was that family could be counted on to show up, to support me, and to believe in me even when I didn't believe in myself. They were all skeptical when I initially started this sentence, wondering if the early changes in me were for real. There was no reason to believe anything I said or did wasn't a scam to get money for something I needed or wanted.

I told my mom, "This wasn't your fault, it was mine."

That was my first adult statement. I had hated my mother and blamed her for having me when she didn't want me. I thought God hated me because I felt as though I had been put on this earth only to suffer. I would need to work on my relationship with God, too.

I believe my mom and dad were both overwhelmed by my imprisonment, but my dad did things differently than my mom. He was supportive of me but more matter of fact about it. He had the attitude that at least he knew where I was at night, and we didn't have to fight each other since I no longer came home drunk. As an adult, I got to know my dad. It turned out he was a cool guy. He would meet and get to know the guys I associated with in prison, and he liked them. This allayed some of his fears for my safety.

When Dad would come up for a visit and see my buddies Mark or J.J., they would come over and talk to him for a while. Dad would send me packages at Christmas back when we could get homemade goodies and tell me to give J.J. some fruitcakes and Mark some cheesecakes. My dad felt that I was safe was because he trusted the guys who I had around me.

As I have stated earlier, I was never a popular kid in school, and that would be the case in prison as well. Being antisocial worked for me, at least a little bit. It meant I didn't trust anyone, and because I spoke so little, nobody knew what I was thinking. I could blend in with the other scowling faces. Although never popular, I saw the wisdom of having at least one or two friends. It was hard to blindly trust someone, but I had seen how some of the guys around me had acted in crisis situations and felt that casting my lot with them was a safe way to go. They had all been in the prison system for years and were able to show me the ropes. Many were tattoo artists and had influence with other groups. The more interactions we had with each group, the more we got to know them and maintain better relationships.

It had taken a couple of years to fully detox from the effects of alcohol. As I got further and further away from alcohol my brain became clearer. My reasoning and problem-solving skills began to improve. Alcohol was no longer my issue in prison, but I would continue to get jammed (high) on any available substance. Thankfully, with each passing year, I enjoyed it less and less.

As my head began to clear, I started to realize that I had morals, values, and integrity. Where the hell did they come from? I make light of it now, but at the time it really troubled me finding this out because I was living in an environment where morality is a weakness.

The relationship with my parents began to change when one day unexpectedly they asked, "What do you need from us?" It was a benign question, but the implications were huge. They were asking my opinion and appeared ready to listen.

I told them, "Listen, I know I have gotten in trouble since going to prison, but what I need from you is to know that sometimes things happen here that shouldn't happen, and they can't always be avoided. I will stay out of trouble wherever I can, and I will try to do the right thing. I need you to support my decisions even if they seem contrary to logic. I need you to trust my judgment." From that day forward my folks never questioned how I was acting in prison. With each passing year they had more reason to trust my actions and decisions. It would take time as I was only in my early twenties and just beginning the process of growing up.

These conversations had never taken place in our home. Now, my parents would come to accept the way I spoke because I was open and honest. We would be able to talk on any subject. With my dad, this would usually be archaeology since he was a geologist and an amateur archaeologist. For Mom, it would usually be books and authors. She and I became close enough to debate issues and argue our positions without getting ticked off at each other. It was fun at the time, and years later I would use these same arguments to win debates in Toastmasters. I remember about six years ago, my lawyer told me, "You and your mother have the same speech patterns." Hopefully, that was a compliment? It means that I have learned to interact in the world of adults.

For all the drama I attached to Mom and Dad early on, I came to appreciate them as an adult and wish they were here today. This is not surprising, as the sentiment is universal, but sometimes it takes a while to learn these lessons. One amazing thing happened around this time, which wasn't prison related and I never saw coming. My mother became a football fan with the arrival of Tom Brady to the New England Patriots. This was so unanticipated because it was so unlike her. At first, I found it humorous, but she stayed with it and got to know the players, plays, defensive schemes, coaches, and the schedules. We would speak on the phone the day after the game and break down what happened. This became our weekly bonding exercise that I really came to value. My mom has now been gone for several years and after every game I still want to call her and talk about it.

One time, very early on in my sentence, I called my dad and tried to scam money from him. I lied that I had gotten into debt playing cards and needed to pay a bill.

Dad said, "Son, that's why you have a knife. I won't tell your mother you called."

He was telling me plainly that we were not doing it this way, it was time to grow up. That was the best lesson my dad ever taught me. I took it to heart and never tried to do anything like that again.

Dad and I had become estranged during my teen years, and I can't say if it was because we were two alpha males butting heads, if we were too much alike (although I don't see it), or if it was simply due to the alcohol, as he was an active alcoholic at the time. My father did end up getting sober and stayed that way for over twenty years. Unfortunately, he would miss seeing more positive changes in my life. He died in 2004 due to complications after heart surgery.

We were told the surgery went well, but late that night the stitches attaching his aorta to his heart let go, and he had a massive bleed out. We were told he would be brain dead if we left him attached to the machines, so we decided as a family to remove life support. It was Mom's decision, but the entire family was on board. We had all discussed end-of-life and quality-of-life decisions and had no arguments against it. I am thankful we didn't have the infighting that so many families have on these issues. I can't say what anyone else's views are on death or ghosts, but my dad's energy was strongly with me for at least a week after his death. When I talked to my brother, he said he felt the same way.

The only thing I can suggest is that my father was trying to give me the sense that thing would be okay, and he would always be there for me.

These changing relationships would occur over the first ten years of my sentence. My sister Denise, the oldest sibling, was in some ways my main support at first. The reader may wonder how that can be based on the way I have described her. During my teen years I was distanced from my brother and sisters while I was running amok. Denise had gotten her life together and was working at the Department of Youth Services (DYS) in Worcester, Massachusetts, as an administrator. This was juvenile lockup. She was not sympathetic to their situations. Then she got married and had her first child after I returned from California and before I came to prison. She had straightened out for approximately 15 years. Denise seemed to prosper and be on a good path. Soon she was also raising her three children (Jillian, Ashley, and Justin). I don't know much about her marriage or if she was happy because we never spoke of such things. Her struggle with addiction issues may have made her sympathetic to mine.

When I came to prison, she was living as well as she ever would, and she felt deeply for me. We had always shared a bond as the "bad" ones in the family. When I got convicted, she seemed to feel for me in a way that Val or Jon couldn't. She brought my nieces and nephew to visit a couple times. My nephew Justin was running around as a toddler but had not yet figured out the concept of solid objects. He would get a full head of steam and go crashing into walls, chairs, and vending machines. When he fell to the ground, he was totally bewildered as to what had happened. My nieces were cute and well behaved.

During her marriage, Denise appeared to be happy and functional but then life started to unravel. She began to tell me that she couldn't bring my nieces or nephew to visit anymore. She said that her and her husband had decided it was in the kids' best interest not to be exposed to prison. I can't tell anyone how to parent their children, and on one level I understood not wanting to take children to a prison. From my side of the table the opinion that Uncle Jeff was an embarrassment and a murderer led to huge feelings of shame as to who I was.

I couldn't tell Denise she was wrong about this, but it hurt me because I felt the decision was a personal rejection. My sister's visits decreased, and her marriage developed problems. I don't know how long their relationship was on the rocks or how long Denise had been using drugs again, but the situation was coming to a head. The marriage crumbled, and Denise started selling heroin; she was caught, arrested, and sent to prison.

Incarceration broke my sister. In prison, she saw a psychiatrist who I believe diagnosed her with depression. It seemed that once she had an excuse for the miseries in her life, she completely gave up. She would never work again and would never find the resilience in life to keep getting up and fighting. I also think her mental health issues were progressing. That was sad because she was never able to be happy, excited, serene, or engaged in life again. Many people in prison have the same issues stemming from long-term depression. Mental health problems existed on my dad's side of the family, and over the years I have questioned my own sanity. After careful consideration I declare myself to be sane!

One of the questions that my sister raised resonates with me: What are the effects of prison on children? This question baffles psychologists, psychiatrists, social workers, and child advocates. We have generation after generation coming to prison, and generation after generation of kids who are coming to prison to see Mom or Dad in the visiting rooms. Can they expect better in life than to have a prison cell waiting for them when they become adults? I may only be a layperson, but shouldn't we aspire as a nation to do better for those people unfortunate enough to be processed through the prison system? Why are prisons the one place where turning out a faulty product is acceptable to society?

Now, turning to Val and Jon and our changing relationships. I had never been completely estranged from them even as we grew distant during our teen years. We never hated each other, we just were not that close. We did not have that kind of family. I'm certain that I hurt each member of the family in different ways, but I don't think I completely alienated Val or Jon. When I came to prison, we were not as close as we should have been, but over the years that would change.

Val and Jon had seen enough of my actions during my teen years to be scarred forever, but they didn't cast me off completely. We would need the next decade just to get to know each other as adults. My siblings had reservations about how I was acting, and they needed time to see for themselves whether my growing up was an act or sincere. It has now been decades, and they have seen the way my life has changed. My interactions with them have changed, and my interactions with the world have changed. I can understand anyone's reluctance to accept a character shift on faith. That is fine, but as this book goes on, you will begin to understand.

Prior to coming to prison, I had nothing but disdain for my fellow humans, so when I entered prison, I not only had to learn how to speak to others, but I also needed to learn how to set my own boundaries. Machiavellian politics (the ability to manipulate and use whatever means necessary to gain power) rule in prison and trying to navigate that without crashing can be tough. Everyone in prison knew each other while I knew no one. I had never been social, so when I came to prison and needed to be at least marginally social, it was tough. I don't want to dwell on prison politics because it is all negative. A life term in maximum security and life in medium security are vastly different. In the max I lived under siege, in medium I don't. In the medium security prison, I try to stay focused on the present rather than living in the past. This eventually became a dominant theme in my life.

My relationships with Val and Jon matured with time and experience, and we are all better off for it. As life has dealt us obstacles to overcome, we have grown closer. We are now bonded in experience rather than just through blood. We have shed tears and come to appreciate each other as adults in ways we couldn't as kids.

The last relationship that changed was my relationship to books. I never read prior to prison, but after taking college classes and realizing how ignorant I was, I began to read, to learn, to study, and to understand. Books allowed me to process information in a way that made sense. Now I wanted to know everything and began reading everything I came across: Physics, Epigenetics, History, Biology, Sociology, etc...

When I came to prison, it was as though I had swapped out a parent who was indifferent to me for a system who was indifferent to me. Call it transference if you want, but psychologically it was just another authority entity trying to control me. I was naive enough to believe that when you go to prison, that IS the punishment, but I would learn that when you come to prison it is FOR punishment, or at least that was the attitude of the administration and the Governor who wanted us to break rocks.

In looking back on almost 40 years in prison, I can tell you first-hand that keeping your foot on someone's throat only makes them angry and unable to breathe (sometime in America it can be lethal as we learned with the death of George Floyd). I believe when people are supported and encouraged rather than torn down and degraded, the results are much better for everyone.

The question is, "Are people redeemable?" I suggest they are. I have seen it many times in men I have known who have never returned to prison after being released. Can anyone who has been in long-term segregation come out improved? My answer is "no." Unless they make a concerted effort to better themselves.

In hindsight, I can tell the reader what was going on between 1984 and 2004 with the prison administration. Now, looking back, it is easy to see that the administration could be defined as "Luddites." They were fearful of technology and unwilling or unable to accept change.

As those administrative employees eventually retired, they were slowly replaced by people who were comfortable with technology and became computer savvy. This new generation would be more willing to exploit new technologies. This was both a blessing and a curse. On the positive side, it let us take advantage of recent technologies like music tablets that had been unimaginable just a couple of years earlier. Tablets did not have internet access but did allow us to access music applications. Access to tablets meant that we had choice in the music we could buy or access. I could now listen to my Louisiana artists who are not played on East Coast radio, like Lucinda Williams, Mindi Abair, Trombone Shorty, Anders Osborn, and Tab Benoit. The downside of this technology is that it monetizes prisoners. Our families are some of the least able to afford them.

The D.O.C would also bring in video visits on kiosks versus in-person or telephone visits. This would again be a blessing and a curse. The positive side was that I could see and speak to my brother who I had not seen in years. Seeing a loved one is quite different than a telephone call. This would have been great for my elderly mother as her health deteriorated year after year and would have allowed her to still have visits. The downside is that the machines frequently don't work, and no one seems willing to service them. One other negative side effect of this technology is that the guards (at the max) were now equipped with technology, too. They would go into the computer databases and pull out guys' cases and then put it out on the block who was in on sex crimes or who had ratted, and it would cause prisoners to be attacked. In other cases, it caused the guards to be attacked for trying to get people seriously hurt or killed. This was probably the number one reason for assaults while I was there.

Chapter 5

Systemic Changes

Acceptance of what has happened is the first step to overcoming the consequences of any misfortune.
—William James

After six years in prison, my emotional maturity was beginning to catch up with my chronological age. I was now clear-headed and had graduated college. The reader may think that all was well, but I still had authority issues and would return to the hole frequently for assaultive behavior.

I almost always worked in prison. I liked to keep busy and out of trouble. When I went out to industries, I worked in the plate shop making license plates, just like in every bad prison movie ever made. It was dirty work, and the temperament of the men on each crew could make for volatile situations. I started out feeding plates into the press, which was very boring, so I would move to the back of the machine where the operator was responsible for changing the dies in the press according to series numbers. I had one other job in the plate shop before moving to a different shop where I worked on the blanker machine. This usually had a better work crew because the guys would earn their way from the presses to the blanker.

The 1990s were a terrible time to be in prison. It was a bad scene on the national level, and as federal policies trickled down, we as prisoners were on the receiving end. Inner-city violence was ravaging American society due to crack cocaine. Politicians were selling fear of "super-predators" and enacting three-strikes laws that would dominate the prison landscape for a generation. Crack cocaine laws were imposed as the government was intent on trying to punish its way out of problems. Joe Biden and Bill Clinton would enact the A. E. D. P. A.

(Anti-terrorism and Effective Death Penalty Act), which would be the most far-reaching piece of criminal legislation to ever be enacted. It all but stopped habeas corpus for prisoners arguing their cases. It created dozens of penalties that could now carry a life sentence. The U.S.

Supreme Court would decide a case called _Sandin v. Connor_, which said in part that the court's job was not to micro-manage the prison system. It signaled to the states that they could do anything they wanted, and the high court would not look at it. This was a substantial change because prior to that, the court was considered to be the last refuge of oversight for prisoner right issues.

The federal government would also begin a massive prison building boom that would last a decade and which the states would follow. To house all the three-strikes victims and all the super-predators, they would need to build prison cells. They not only built prison cells, but also convinced everyone for the need to build supermax prisons. To those who do not know, supermax prisons are prisons, inside of prisons, and they consist of mostly of segregation cells where they sent prisoners for decades at a time, often on very serious charges.

This was not like a court of law, as the burden of proof is simply that it was more likely than not that something happened. Other guards would assess the guard's word as to credibility versus the word of a convicted inmate. I will leave it to the reader to determine an outcome in these situations.

The federal government also began the process of privatizing prisons on a grand scale. The net result of this was that the people writing legislation to keep prisoners in jail would now become major stockholders in companies that were profiting by keeping them there. Does this seem right? As the policies that were being enacted on the federal level began to trickle down, this is how that looked on the state level.

State politics at the time were also pushing the fear of crime. The governor's office at that time was occupied by William Weld ("Let's reintroduce prisoners to the joys of busting rocks") and by Paul Argeo Cellucci ("Why should felons have the right to vote?").

Paul Argeo Cellucci amended the State Constitution to eliminate a prisoner's right to vote. In my opinion, Cellucci never let the facts stand in the way of politics. He sold the public a bill of goods about how prisoners were trying to sway local elections. But the truth was that we never would have been able to do so. The only way we could vote was by absentee ballot in the towns where we were living while arrested.

The D.O.C. (Department of Correction) was under Human Services rather than public safety, as it is now. Under Human Services, the D.O.C. had to go to the Statehouse each year to seek funding. Merging the guards' union with the state police union not only strengthened the public safety union but also made it automatically funded.

One of the first things enacted under public safety was to restrict the press. Any statement that would be released came from the D. O. C. 's press agent. Prior to this, the press had access to prisoners even if just by phone. Is a press statement more truthful than a first-hand account? Why should the D.O.C. fear a free press?

Prisons had avocations in which men could practice their woodworking and leather working trades. Men could order their own material, sell their wares, and make money learning both valuable work skills and the value of capitalism. Isn't this what they should be doing? Well, after the press were told by the guards' union that prisoners were making more money than the guards, the avocations were taken as well.

Prisons offered art courses, and for just the cost of pens and paint, the men had a creative outlet, and some were extremely talented. The guys could sell their works in New York and earn income.

One time a serial killer put up pieces for auction, and the press heard about it and said he was trying to profit from his crime. Well, the work they showed had nothing to do with his crime, but panic and outrage ensued, leading to legislation against this. I will not try to defend the actions of a serial killer, but could this have resulted from the hysteria developing in the press at the time?

When I came to prison, prisoners could receive furloughs. This meant that based on good behavior, men could earn increasingly more time to spend with their families or loved ones. It might start at a few hours but could eventually become 24, 48, or 72 hours depending on how often someone successfully completed their furloughs. Eventually, Willie Horton committed new crimes while Mike Dukakis was running for president, and it became a bad political commercial about the revolving door in and out of the prison system. The fact was that it was a successful program for years before it was taken away.

Creative writing courses were removed for no apparent reason, and that only entailed a pad of paper. I guess the idea of people having creative ideas was threatening to them.

Each prison had banquets in which the Irish, Italian, black people, bikers, religious, Spanish, and others could order catered food and participate in cultural bonding in a positive manner. This would usually involve getting pizzas or something like that, but it was taken away as well.

Our families used to be able to send us clothes, sheets, towels, sneakers, razors, and other personal items. These gave way to prison clothes and the requirement to wear prison IDs.

The prisons were being broken down into smaller and smaller segments. Instead of the whole prison going to the yard at the same time, the administration organized it into maximum end and minimum end, with the two sides unable to interact. Then it was configured into gang blocks versus non-gang blocks. Eventually they would only allow one block at a time in the yard. Sometimes it would only be one tier at a time or a couple cells at a time. In theory, this was so that it would be easier to regain control in case of a riot. What it was in fact was that the states were getting funding for gang blocks because the feds had told them we were all gang members and super predators.

Walpole was no exception. They built a departmental disciplinary unit with shiny segregation cells, and they needed to justify it. The problem was that we didn't have enough gang members to justify this monstrosity, so the D. O. C. created gangs by simply snatching guys up that had gotten into multiple person conflicts and declared them a gang. This allowed them to create white gangs, which justified the funding but served the secondary function of muting claims of discrimination by the black people and Spanish guys who were being targeted.

It may be hard to imagine now, but we used to be considered men. By this I mean that if our jobs required it, we could walk around in maximum security with hammers, chisels, and pliers, and no one thought anything about it. We had to do a tool accountability at the end of the day, of course. No one would use a tool from work as a weapon because if you did you would never work again.

We could receive phone calls from anyone who would accept our calls or get visits from anyone coming by to see us when they were in the area, assuming they could be cleared to enter the facility. Now, our visits and phone calls are severely restricted, and you must fill out pages of intrusive questions to be allowed in. Most people receive fewer visits and phone calls as a result.

Last, we were able to receive Pell grants, which allowed us to take college courses. I will just say this: education is one of the big keys to allowing people to raise themselves and their families out of poverty and put them on the road to advancement and pride in themselves. Community college is far cheaper than prison, and society gets far more bang for the buck. College students are also the least likely to re-offend, being willing to put forth the effort is probably a sign that someone may be trying to better his position.

It was against this backdrop that I was trying to choose a different path. I stated before that books were my safe place, and when I would go to segregation, I would read from sunup until late at night. In 1990 or 1991, I was once again in segregation for assaulting a guard. I had also been severely depressed and was on the verge of suicide. I was now about 30 years old and saw absolutely no future. I knew that I could not continue on this path of just going into and out of the hole, getting beat up every time in the process. I would read the Koran, the Bible, and the Torah. I recognized quotes that I hadn't known were from these books. But the concept of God that they described didn't register with me because each claimed exclusivity to the truth. I would read philosophy and come across Nietzsche and the concept of the superman as well as the destruction of the earth to rebuild. I read Machiavelli and learned the concept of throwing myself into the gears of the machine just to jam it up (wasn't that what I was doing?). I read Plato, Aristotle, and all the Stoics.

Eventually I came across the likes of Hobbs, Locke, Emerson, Thoreau, and others. I read about good government, civil disobedience, and the social contract, but it was Henry David Thoreau's *On Walden Pond* that made me ask myself, "*Now that I am in the hole away from others, what does my life look like? What kind of man am I?*" It was the first time that I had done a searching and thorough moral inventory of myself. What I found was that I didn't like the person I had become. I saw all my faults and defects of character. I had never seen anything good about myself or anything in my life, but this time it was different because I knew that I could change at least some aspects of myself. Philosophy always poses moral questions, and when I read it, I knew that the inner me had some of these good qualities that had been buried so deeply that I couldn't access them when they were smothered under alcohol and drugs.

I also tried to understand the mindset of the policymakers and legislators who wrote the policies about prison. I suppose that like all bureaucracies, the people at the top only know how things work by books, and they have no idea how their policies impact the people they are supposedly looking out for.

My mind was in turmoil, and I began to study art and artists and found that I was drawn to the odd and bizarre because it was more in keeping with my environment. That style at least made me feel *something.* I liked the Dali's, Brueghel's, Bosche's, Escher's, H.R. Geiger's, Rene Magritte's, Klimt's and K. Lee's. I even tried to understand why a Mondrian would have such value when it was just patterns of shapes and colors. The Manets and Monets, Renoirs, Rembrandts, Caravaggio's and Titian's didn't seem to speak to me, but then all of a sudden, I would come across Albrecht Durer, and it would suddenly make sense. I needed to read and process what I had read and think about it for a long time. In the end, I seldom agreed with art critics, but I liked the works that appealed to me emotionally. They say that art is subjective, and beauty is in the eye of the beholder, and that was true to me as well.

When I was in the hole contemplating suicide, I received a book called the *Tao Te Ching* by Lao Tzu translated by Ursula Leguin. It wasn't the first time I had read this type of book, but on that day a passage stood out, it was titled "Paradoxes":

Nothing in the world is as soft, as weak, as water.

Nothing else can wear away the hard, the strong, and remain unaltered.

Soft overcomes hard, weak overcomes strong. Everybody knows it, nobody uses the knowledge. The wise say by bearing common defilements you become a sacrifice at the altar of earth.

By bearing common evils you become a lord of the world.

Right words sound wrong.

At the time I was headed toward suicide, this passage pulled me from the edge. I still have a copy of the book thirty years later. What it meant to me at the time was that the hardness of the

prison didn't need to break me. I could be as the water and overcome the hardness and defilements of incarceration. Until that time in my life, I had not encountered much Eastern philosophy except for *The Prophet* by Khalil Gibran. This concept dominated my mindset in the two years that followed. Would yoga have appealed to me if I hadn't been exposure to Buddhism and mindfulness? I can't say for sure.

What it conveyed to me immediately was that I could attempt to be less obnoxious and abrasive, less confrontational and defiant. It would take a while to learn how to implement this in my life, but the seed had been planted. That is also my way of learning, where I need to mull over a certain concept until it just clicks for me, and I figure out how to implement it.

I gravitated toward these books because in a prison setting, the more comfortable you can become with the concept of giving ground to gain ground, you can learn to meet resistance with surrender and gain power through ceding power, the better off you will be.

By not allowing the guards to influence my reaction, I was beginning to empower myself. That was the beginning of my walking in the light.

I went on to study all kinds of Buddhist teachings, self-help books, books on mindfulness, breathing, and yoga, but it would take time to fully embrace the concepts. When it came to spirituality, I was very reluctant to embrace it, but eventually I did.

If there were any programs in the maximum-security facility, I wasn't aware of them because no one that I knew was participating in such programs. Maximum security was not a place of enlightenment and acceptance, it was a place of violence and predation. Almost everyone I knew in there were lifers. Lifers had no hope and no out-dates, so there was no reason to enroll in programs if they were offered. There was no talk about people getting paroled or self-improvement. The guys were not talking about becoming better people or helping their neighbors. They were talking about whose turn it was to make the knives.

They were talking about who did what to whom and trying to figure out a way to get high for the day.

I could understand this position. I have been that guy waiting for drugs, lying in bed eating chips and waiting for something to happen just to break the monotony of prison life. Contrary to movie depictions, prison is not usually a highly active place. Most of the time it is mind-numbing routine.

My mom continued to visit every week. We would sit and talk and began to get along and be civil to each other. One thing that happened that none of us saw coming was that my dad would be diagnosed with depression and was put on medication. In his case, it worked wonders. He had an inner personality that none of us ever knew about, and he even told jokes from time to time. The turnabout was amazing. Our entire family couldn't believe what a drastic change occurred in him, and we all began to not only embrace him more, but we also began to become something resembling a normal family. Although we had been so utterly dysfunctional for years, we all desired to connect as relatives.

The rest of the 1990's and early 2000 's were mostly spent working. I went on to other jobs working in the warehouse and driving the forklift. This was the job that was the most fun because it allowed me to feel human. There would be other work, though, and I did everything from clerk jobs, to assembling furniture, to making brushes.

In the year 2000, I was transferred to Shirley Prison, which had become the new max facility. Walpole was relegated to the processing of new men only. The DDU still existed in Walpole, but the prison only had a small cadre of workers remaining there. By 1995 things had tilted so far against prisoners and prison rights issues that it was hard to see any hope on the horizon.

In retrospect, and somewhat apart from the prison system, there were beginning to be voices in the wilderness pushing for juvenile justice. In particular, changes related to life without parole for juvenile offenders.

One of those advocates was secretary of state Madelaine Albright who in 1995 entered into a treaty by the UNITED NATIONS CONVENTION ON THE RIGHTS OF CHILDREN. Which in article 37 (a) provides that neither capital punishment nor life in prison without the possibility of parole shall be imposed for offenses committed by a person below 18 years of age. This treaty was signed but never ratified so it doesn't have the force of law. It was however instructive because it speaks to what the international community believes the standards of children's welfare should be and what is and is not acceptable when it comes to our children.

In 2005, Roper v. Simmons 543 U.S 551 was decided. This decision stated that capital punishment was unconstitutional for people under 18 years of age. While neither of these two things would directly affect juveniles in Massachusetts, it was the beginning of a very subtle shift which would rock the courts and the prison system in the coming years.

My buddy Billy who is pretty knowledgeable about the law told me in 2005 after the Roper decision that the court was going to abolish life without the possibility of parole for juvenile offenders, but we all thought he was nuts. Then, in 2010, we were both in Norfolk when Graham v Florida 560 U.S. 48, 79 (2010) was decided. In this case the court determined that life without the possibility of parole was unconstitutional for persons under 18 years of age, convicted of crimes other than homicide (I would ask why it was ever legal to give someone under 18 a life without parole sentence for a non- homicide case?) this kicked the can down the road just a little bit further.

Finally, in a case called Miller v. Alabama and Jackson v. Hobbs 132 S.Ct.

2455 (2012) the court decided it was unconstitutional for states to mandate life without parole for individuals under 18 years of age, including cases of homicide. This was a huge decision. It meant that many juveniles who had been sentenced to slow death (life without parole) would now become parole eligible. They now had hope of one day getting out and picking up the pieces of their broken lives. These men had done decades in prison with me and none of them had any hope of ever getting out of prison prior to this decision.

The men who I had known for decades were now grown men of 40, 50, and 60 years age. They were no longer the rambunctious, impetuous, Impulsive reactionary knuckleheads they were when they came to prison. Most of them had grown up, matured, had more life experience and regretted the choices and decisions they had made in life.

They had come to see and acknowledge the harm and destruction they had caused.

The victim was dead, their family devastated. We were in prison, our families devastated. All of our communities were devastated as the ripple effects of our crimes filter outwards.

I can't speak to what brought each individual to prison, but I can tell the reader that in almost every case where someone I know was involved in a homicide they had looked long and hard at the decisions that landed them in prison. How it happened. Why it happened. What happened.

It was now the medical and scientific communities which were driving the court's decisions because the brain science surrounding juveniles had progressed so far due to new medical technologies. The brain science continues to evolve, and we now have long-term longitudinal studies that were lacking ten years ago. There is a reason juveniles act different than adults and I will address that in an upcoming chapter.

As I close this chapter I will just state that most of us at 40, 50, 60 years of age are no longer the people (children) we were at 18 and hopefully we have grown, matured, taken responsibility and learned how to act like civilized people. This is as true for Lifers as it is for members of society.

These court decisions leading to the changes in life without parole were led by science, so the question becomes if the brain science applies to the next group of young offenders, 18-21, shouldn't they get relief, too? There are now 10 years of studies that shows the brain science applies to the next group of individuals. The court's reluctance to address this is understandable but should youthful offenders be punished for having undeveloped brains?

After 2005, the D.O.C. changed a classification policy to a points-based system, and because I had very few points, I was told that I would be moving soon. That would come in 2007, when they told me, "Pack it up, you're going to Norfolk."

I was ready for this move, but it is always hard to relocate because you lose friendships that you spent years building. I left my friend Billy behind. I would be going to a new environment where I would have to forge new friendships and alliances. When you go to a new prison, you never know if you are walking into problems. One of your friends may have stabbed one of their friends or visa-versa. Fortunately, that didn't happen.

Chapter 6

Smelling the Roses and Learning Spanish

In 2007 I was transferred to Norfolk state prison after spending almost twenty-three years in maximum security. Norfolk is a level-four prison which is just a security designation but does not tell the reader anything about it as prisons can vary. Norfolk is a very soft level-four where stabbings and major violence are almost unheard of. Guys may still get high, get drunk and go to the hole, but by and large there are few major problems. This was a very welcome change after living under siege in the max for so long. It would take several years to get acclimated to this new environment.

Upon arrival at Norfolk, I was processed through the new man section and placed in a holding cell in the hospital wing pending release to population. As men would come by the holding cell, the first thing I noticed was that they all looked so healthy. They were tanned by the sun, and all looked to be in shape. Everyone from the max was usually ghostly pale from never getting any sun, and 30 - 40 pounds overweight because they were always locked down and never got out for exercise.

It felt so good to be in a new environment where I could go to the yard, walk all day, stay outside and simply feel the sun on my face again. This was so welcome after spending decades living under siege in the max. When I first arrived here, I was really thrown off by the lack of negative energy and the lack of tension between groups of people. I knew that I had PTSD (Post Traumatic Stress Disorder) from spending that much time in the max and that it was going to be quite an adjustment, but I was ready for whatever changes I would encounter.

Norfolk is a very old prison and looks more like a college campus than a prison. Once you enter through the main gate you are immediately facing a big administrative building. Off to the left leads a paved walkway which heads towards the visiting center. The walkways to the administrative building and the visiting center are covered in flowers and it looks like something out of the Wizard of Oz as Dorothy goes through the poppy fields. Once you go through the administration building you enter the internal part of the prison where it really begins to look like a campus.

There is a centrally located quad with housing units on the east and west sides. On the south end is the O.I.C. (Officer in Charge) building which is a two-story structure which contains the law library and general library on the first floor and school rooms on the he second floor. The school rooms also double as function rooms for programs. On the north end is the auditorium which also has several rooms for religious programs and assorted functions. Shooting off from the quad are alley ways that lead to the east and west sides of the camp. On the east side is three more housing units, a track, baseball field, hand ball courts, a basketball court and a walkway down to the gymnasium. On the west side is several more housing units, a bigger track, two basketball courts, a soccer field and several tables and benches.

In front of each housing unit are flower beds that some of the men put a lot of time and effort into maintaining. Gladiolas, azaleas, marigolds, irises, tulips, roses and plants of every size, shape and description. When I first arrived at Norfolk, I would wander into each garden literally and figuratively and stop to smell the roses, to touch the texture of the plants and simply contemplate how thoroughly and completely I had been kept apart from nature for decades. It is very unnatural to have no contact with Mother Earth for that amount of time. I had not seen or smelled a flower for twenty-three years with the exception of the occasional dandelion. The guys maintaining the gardens and the guards working the yard may not have appreciated my stomping around in the flower beds, but I would not be deterred. The cops would see me and just tell me to keep it moving and when they didn't receive a negative reaction from me, they just let me be. They know who the new guys on the camp are and one of them might just occasionally ask me how long it has been? I would tell them 23 years and they would just shake their heads and tell me don't be too long.

The conversations in the yard were different than in the max as were the attitude of the people. Instead of everyone being suited up and ready to jump (armed and prepared for battle) they seemed relaxed and friendly towards each other. This was very unsettling to me because I had lived under siege for so long. In a sense I was very glad to be in this new environment, but it took some getting used to. The conversations in the yard were about doing programs, finding a job, staying busy, staying out of the mix (illegal things) and finding ways to occupy your time. Guys were even talking about investing in the stock market, buys, puts, drip funds, mutual funds, reverse stock splits, portfolios etc. It was like hearing a new language and I was intrigued. I was amazed that prisoners could invest in the markets and all they required was your money. At the time prisoners were able to invest freely but since then the D.O.C. has stopped allowing us to send money out. They justify everything by saying we may be investing in illegal drugs or businesses. A policy exists that says we simply need to show the money is not for illegal purposes, but they use it as a blanket denial to any request.

Most of the guys I knew at Norfolk were all lifers and when I got here after not seeing these guys for many years, they had all matured, no longer acted like knuckleheads and were all engaged in positive things. When I arrived at Norfolk lifers were not being allowed into programs but within a couple of years the juvenile offenders would be seeing the parole board. Suddenly the parole board wanted these guys in programs, their lawyers wanted them in programs and reluctantly the D.O.C. relented and began letting lifers into groups.

There is usually an official way of doing something and then there is a much better, more practical way of doing things that gets much more accomplished. I wanted to do the master's program in the college but was told that it no longer existed. As of this writing once the last class of college students graduate there will no longer be a degree program at Norfolk. They are moving to a certificate program only, which will effectively end the long and proud tradition of college education programs at Norfolk. That is truly a shame as a college degree has the highest rate of success against recidivism. Everyone who I knew was working or doing programs and had found ways to occupy their time in a positive manner.

Then, one day, when I was talking to my friends, I stated that I needed something to occupy my mind and my time, I half-jokingly suggested that I could learn a language. Instead of laughing at me, they said, "Why don't you speak to Jaime?"

"Who is Jaime?" I asked, "He has been tutoring the guys from Boston University with all their subjects, and he speaks Spanish," they said.

Not long after that I met Jaime. We took some laps on the track while talking about education, the max experience, and what I was hoping to do now that I was out of max.

"Why do you want to learn Spanish?" he asked, pausing to catch his breath.

I related to him a story about my neighbor and me in Ten Block. We had been playing chess through the bars for weeks on end by making separate chess-boards with squares numbered one through sixty-four and calling out which piece would be moved to which spot on the board as we couldn't see into each other's cell. After playing for weeks without conflicts, we one day started arguing over a game, and Carlos cursed me under his breath. So, I yelled to him,

"Yo, Carlos, you got something to say to me, say it in English."

Carlos responded, "Why the fuck don't you learn Spanish?"

WHAT?! I wanted to break right through the wall and smash him. I was so mad. I cursed at him. I paced my cell back and forth, back and forth, fuming. After ten minutes of plotting his demise, I banged on his wall.

BANG – BANG – BANG!! "Yo, Carlos!"

"What d'ya want?"

"Yo, Carlos, will you teach me Spanish?" I asked.

Carlos damn near fell down laughing and said, "Yes, we will begin right now."

We started by conjugating verbs that day. Carlos and I never saw each other again

as I left the tier a month later. But the seed to learning Spanish was planted.

Jaime chuckled when I told him this was my start and my inspiration to learn Spanish. He said we could go to the library and study every weekend from 8:30 to 11:30.

"Really?" I asked. I told him at the max facility we couldn't get together in groups of three, or we would be considered a gang.

Jaime laughed and said, "That was the max, but you are at Norfolk now, so drop the max mindset."

"How do I sign up?" I asked.

"There's no signup because it isn't an official group. It's guys getting together to learn on our own. Just bring a good attitude and an open mind."

I had lived with Spanish guys in prison and never considered learning their language until that argument with Carlos. *El tuvo razon!* (He was right!).

Jaime and I began to study in the library and got to know one another. Jaime is a Colombian American and had grown up in both places and he was willing to give his own free time to teach me. I had become so cynical and jaded over the years that I never could have anticipated this offer. I would test the limits of Jaime's patience and his ability to teach as I came to the table in my mid-forties with absolutely no penchant for the language. Some mornings I would seem to grasp it, and the next week I would show up and forget everything. I was forever asking Jaime, "Why? Why? Why?"

He responded, "Necesito ensenarte mas palabras que simplemente - porque, porque, porque." (I need to teach you more words than just -why, why, why).

We came to know each other well and would join many programs together over the years. Jaime is also a lifer, and he was looking for a way to put his time to beneficial use. He took me on as his project. No matter what society may say about murderers, all I can tell you is that, from firsthand experience, this lifer was offering to help someone with nothing asked in return.

I took this lesson to heart and years later would offer to do the same thing for others as a way of paying it forward. This altruism that I would see in other lifers has never been part of the narrative that makes the news when they describe us as savages. It is also part of the reason I decided to not include prison tales of treachery, violence, rape, murder, or suicides. Those concepts are well documented in Hollywood movies and D.O.C. press releases. I wanted to write a different narrative about the changes I have seen in people over the years, the stories of redemption and of people fighting and winning over their personal demons. There are numerous people who get out every year and never come back, but those success stories do not make the headlines..

Our redemption stories are not about famous people of note, they are people of humble origins (poor and uneducated), and when they return to their communities, they return as fathers, sons, uncles, brothers, and grandfathers. If you never hear their names, it is because they are working, paying bills, looking out for their families and doing what they need to do to stay out of prison.

My buddy Billy would show up on the camp about a year later and ended up in my block where we were cellies for a number of years. Most of us in prison don't have very wide social circles so when we are able to reconnect with people that is huge. He is now parole eligible and has been working a job for about 14 years. He is another one who has grown up, matured, and taken ownership of his actions. When the miller decision came down and made him parole eligible, he ran off to do programs as well but he noticed that there was a gap in the programming. They had no program directly dealing with youthful offenders, so he started one from the ground up called the Y.O.C. (Youthful Offender Coalition). He is also very good with the law and is always helping others on the camp with their legal issues. Both of our moms became close over the years and when each of our moms died, we were the ones to lean on each other and support each other through pain and sadness.

Jaime and I had been practicing together for about six months when I met the invisible man. I call him the invisible man because he was invisible to me. Jaime one day asked me a question about one of the clerks in the library and I told him I didn't know who he was talking about. He described him as the little black guy from the Ivory coast. I don't know Jaime. He said, "that little guy that speaks five languages". "I don't know Jaime". So, he says "that guy who went to all the best universities in Europe." Nope. I don't know Jaime. He tried one last time by telling me, "you know the one who owned that engineering firm in France." No Jaime I don't know. A few days later Jaime pointed out the guy to me and I knew exactly who he meant. During the week I began to think of this guy a lot and wondered how he could be so utterly and completely invisible to me. He was obviously very accomplished as he spoke multiple languages, had lived and travelled around the world, had several prestigious degrees and was more successful than I ever thought of being. I didn't like what this was telling me about myself. I pondered on this all week, and I came to some conclusions. The reason this man was invisible to me was because he wasn't a threat to me. For twenty-three years, I had unconsciously assessed everyone on the basis of a personal threat to me and unconsciously I deemed him a "non- threat," a "non-human," a nonentity. This did not sit well with me at all because I had always wanted to be acknowledged, valued, and appreciated as a person and I did the opposite with this guy.

What it did say to me was that I needed to pay more attention to the people around me. How I was assessing people, and how my time in the max had affected my judgement. I could understand how it happened, but I also knew that I needed to address it.

Our little group would grow and fluctuate over time. When guys on the camp heard what we were doing the ones with an interest in learning began to show up. We always had a mix of old and young, educated and not, black, white, Spanish with a few Asians over the years. We had gang bangers and suburban kids, professionals and criminals. It was a very inclusive group and we had nothing in common except a desire to learn. Some days we would do all Spanish work and other days we would have discussions about what people were going to do when released. What had changed in their lives to keep them from returning to prison. We would talk about drug abuse, physical abuse, emotional abuse, sexual abuse and how all of these things contributed to us coming to prison. We would encourage guys to do college courses, toast masters, prison programs and we asked them to look at their lives and their own responsibility in their crimes and the trauma they caused in their communities. Most guys were very open to this informal, relaxed style of learning. We spent several years learning together. After several years, Jaime got a little burnt out and dropped it on me to continue the class without him. By that point I knew how to teach although I lacked some confidence. I told Jaime that I wasn't fluent enough and he would tell me "there may be people more fluent than you, but you know the grammar better than them and that is what they are lacking." Jaime said I am still here if you have questions, but also doing it alone will force you to be a better teacher. And so, I took over the course and had one of my students assist me in the same manner that I had begun assisting Jaime. Some of my students have gotten out of prison and are working as tax paying citizens to this day. That is what a successful change is supposed to look like in someone's life. We always told guys that if you want better results in your lives you need to be the ones to initiate that change.

The classes shut down for a couple years due to Covid but recently we have got up and running again. The faces have changed but the desire to learn, to change and to do something positive have been consistent over time. My belief is that the reason we have success doing this is because we encourage people in what they can do, and we empower them to do it. In contrast to the D.O.C. which tells people what they can't do and strips them of power.

In many ways things in my life were going as well as they could in a prison environment. Doing a life sentence usually means that storm clouds are on the horizon. In this case that would be the slow but steady decline in my mom's health. She had been both the central villain and the source of my strength. She was the primary person responsible for making me who I am, for better or worse. How ironic that the one who wished I was never born would also be the one to show me love, compassion, and understanding in life.

The first ten years I was in prison was spent on just learning to relate to her as an adult, the next ten was spent repairing bridges. By the time my dad died in 2004, my mom and I knew we were on borrowed time, and I think we both made a huge effort to not only get closer but to really begin the process of forgiving each other. I had to get past my anger and forgive her for not being the perfect mom and for not giving me the love I needed. I think in her own way she had to forgive me for being who I am and not fulfilling her ideal of the perfect son. Over the years she had come to believe in me and became my most ardent supporter and I had come to love her and value her as a person in a way that I could not have as a child. We both literally had to grow up in order to respect each other.

My mom had always greatly valued her independence and took great pride in being able to drive out to visit me when she wanted. However, time was working against her. From 2007 until maybe 2011 she could still come visit, buy me some sandwiches, get some photos taken and just spend time together. She was becoming more frail. More of a risk of falling and had broken many bones. She fell once again and shattered her elbow catching MRSA in the hospital. She would be on and off antibiotics depending on whether the MRSA was active or not and would need a wick to drain fluids. She had shrunken by about a foot and was now tiny and frail.

It would fall on Val to care for mom. I could do nothing to help because I had put myself in jail, Denise couldn't be counted on to help with anything due to mental health issues and my brother was always in Hawaii, Iraq, Germany etc., and simply wasn't available. Mom and Val fought like cats and dogs, but they loved each other. I did not envy Val this job because I knew how mean, attacking, judgmental, and unappreciative my mom could be. Val had a life of her own to live and could not be counted on or expected to bring mom up every weekend. The best that I could do was support Val in whatever decisions she made and trust in her judgement. I was fortunate to even have that as many lifers do not. I would get the opportunity to talk to my mom one last time on the phone as someone held it to her ear. I was able to tell her that I loved her and that if it was her time to go then just go. I told her that I would be OK, and that I was now strong enough to stand on my own. She died early the next morning on February 17th, 2014, surrounded by family.

My sister Denise would follow mom a few years later and now it is just me, Val and Jon remaining. I am extremely thankful to have them.

I have now been working in the shipping department for 14 years. I have come to believe that if someone is willing to work in prison in order to buy things from the canteen then he is probably much more prepared to work a job on the street in order to pay bills. Having a concept of work for pay (even if it's not much pay) and developing some kind of work ethic is vital to someone's chances of success on the street. I think most of the guys at work prefer being there than hanging around the block or the yard all day. We come from different places and have different opinions and experiences but at the end of the day we find a way to get along and be supportive of each other even if we don't always agree. I like their company immensely and they help keep me thinking young. Everyday my buddy Ziggy brings such a great attitude and positive energy to the workplace that it is nice to be in that type of environment all day.

Chapter 7

The Law, Appeals, Brain Science and a Look Ahead

Although I had a previous criminal record, for the purposes of this book my introduction to the legal system begins with my arrest in December of 1983. After my arrest I was placed in the House of Correction for six months while awaiting trial. During this period, my lawyer met with me twice, for an hour each time. My relationship with my lawyer was contentious. I felt he didn't take the case seriously, wouldn't do what I asked him to do, and wouldn't introduce evidence that I thought might be useful. During this time, he never explained to me the difference between first-degree murder and second-degree murder. He never told me that I could plead guilty to second degree murder, and he never explained to me the concept of extreme atrocity or cruelty. I did not clearly understand the charges or any recourse I might have to offer in defense.

I knew the evidence against me was overwhelming, and my lawyer said that he would talk to the prosecutor about a manslaughter plea. The lawyer asked the prosecutor about manslaughter many times and was rebuffed by him. Returning to my holding cell, he said that no deal could be reached, and we would be going to trial. I believed that meant we had no other options. I did not know that pleading guilty to a second-decree offense was an option. The trial took place in June of 1984, with me relying on the attorney's legal knowledge and expecting his fair representation of my case.

Two weeks into the trial, my lawyer came to the holding cell where I was waiting and explained the concept of extreme atrocity and cruelty. He said the jury could find me guilty of this even with no weapons or intent. He explained that if I pleaded guilty, I would be eligible for parole in fifteen years, but if the court convicted me, I would be serving a life sentence without parole – a slow death. So, I immediately told him to enter a plea of guilty to second-degree murder.

He returned ten minutes later and told me it was too late because we were two weeks into the trial, and the District Attorney wouldn't allow it. I mention this now because it would later become an issue, which brings me to post-conviction litigation.

Direct Appeal: 1987

On direct appeal we argued the following:

1. The denial of Motion to Sever was prejudicial error, requiring a new trial.

2) The trial judge's failure to ensure the jury was impartial in the wake of exposure to media coverage of alleged reports of jury tampering denied me of the right to a fair trial.

3) The jury instructions as to *diminished capacity due to alcohol consumption* were incorrect.

4) The jury instructions on *malice aforethought* were erroneous.

5) The jury instructions on *joint venture* and its relation to intoxication were incorrect.

6) The verdict should be reduced under Mass General Laws c. 278, s 33E.

Errors Acknowledged by Supreme Judicial Court (SJC) in Direct Appeal Decision:

The SJC acknowledged there was a Bruton violation using the co-defendant's statement against me. However, it was ruled harmless beyond a reasonable doubt. The SJC also acknowledged the publicity surrounding the jury tampering did taint the trial proceedings. It then went on to rule the trial judge was within his discretion to decide the taint was not harmful.

Motion for New Trial: 1986-1989

I filed a "Pro-Se" motion for a new trial in 1986 (action filed by myself without a lawyer) prior to the direct appeal being decided. Once the direct appeal was decided, I amended the motion for a new trial (this time through counsel). We alleged ineffectiveness of counsel, both trial and appellate, on these grounds:

Counsel's failure to fully present the prejudice I suffered because of the denial of the Motion to Sever (separate my case from the co-defendant).

Counsel's failure to move to suppress my statement to police, which was given after invoking my right to counsel.

Failure to present a robust defense regarding how intoxication impacted my ability to act with malice or extreme atrocity or cruelty considering my long-standing, well documented problems with alcohol.

An evidentiary hearing was granted on the new trial motion. Although my appellate attorney had argued on direct appeal that denial of the Motion to Sever was erroneous, the SJC agreed but upheld the conviction on a finding of harmlessness. What my new counsel realized, that my previous counsel had missed, was that my previous counsel never preserved the record or made proper motions to demonstrate the entirety of the harm I suffered as a result of being tried with the co-defendant. The new counsel introduced my affidavit with this motion. This affidavit stated that trial counsel had informed me that no plea was available to me. What is clear from the record is that the District Attorney's office would not offer a manslaughter plea, which was what my trial counsel pushed for. The trial prosecutor through his affidavit has confirmed this. He stated he would have been supportive of such an offer, and he believed his superiors would have been as well. I stated that I would have accepted the offer of a second-degree charge on a plea pre-trial. The first time that trial counsel raised the issue of a plea to second-degree was in the middle of trial, at which point it was too late.

Mass General Law G. L. C. 278, Section 33e Motion and Hearing:

Appellate counsel litigated a Motion for Review under 278, Section 33 E, arguing my trial counsel was ineffective for not taking an interlocutory appeal of the denial of the Motion to Sever and not objecting when co-counsel suggested, through State Police testimony, that a possible manslaughter offer was discussed for the co-defendant immediately before giving a second statement to police. This became the most damning piece of evidence against me. Counsel also argued the Massachusetts statute as to extreme atrocity or cruelty was void for vagueness.

Error Acknowledged by the Single Justice:

The single justice ruled although the ineffective assistance claim put forward introduced a "new source of error" to this case, the error committed by trial counsel, when viewed within the context of the entire trial, did not affect the verdict. So, we had three acknowledged errors at this point of post-conviction appeals.

Petition for Writ of Habeas Corpus and Appeals: 1995-98

During this time, I had a new appellate counsel who argued error as to the Motion to Sever, error in the jury instructions as to malice, and ineffective assistance of counsel due to failure to object to the faulty malice instructions. The petition was denied in 1997. One issue counsel looked at was whether trial counsel was ineffective for failing to engage in plea negotiations. Despite trial counsel's testimony at the new trial motion hearing stating that he engaged the prosecutor (Attorney Aloise) in plea negotiations numerous times to no avail, appellate counsel obtained an affidavit confirming that no negotiations for a plea to second-degree murder were attempted by trial counsel. The plea negotiations centered on a manslaughter plea only.

Marino

In 2013, the SJC decided *Commonwealth v. Marino* 464 Mass 115. For the first time, the SJC stated there is a specific duty on the part of defense counsel to advocate for a client through plea negotiations for a disposition that is materially better than what the client can receive as punishment after trial. Failure to do so amounts to deficient performance on the part of counsel. *Marino* would at this point become a claim. Although I would not become aware of this *Marino* claim for years, it would give me standing to raise the claim with new counsel in 2015.

When I was shot down on my federal habeas corpus appeal in 1995, that marked the end of the road for my legal options at that point. The only way I could get relief was if there was a change in the law or if there was some newly discovered evidence. With no options left I completely gave up and resigned myself to dying in prison (life without parole).

With no hope of ever getting out, I needed to focus on simply existing in prison. With nothing to look forward to or hope for I needed to let go of any hopes or dreams I was hanging onto. When I first came to prison, I used to have dreams of flying all the time. After I was shot down my dreams began to change. Instead of flying over the prison walls and trees and above lakes and the freedom beyond, I kept having more trouble flying over the prison walls and my wings began to get caught up in concertina wire, until eventually the dreams just stopped. I knew it was my minds way of trying to process my lack of hope in the world. I would be stuck here until I die. I knew this was a significant event in my life because it meant that I could not do a life sentence dreaming about what would never happen for me in the free world.

I would still miss and dream about things in the world, like diving into a pond on a hot summer day, a black raspberry ice cream cone smothered in jimmies (chocolate sprinkles), puppies, fishing, a pretty girl in a sun dress, etc. but I could no longer afford the delusion of one day being free. I would surround myself with other lifers doing 1st degree sentences (life without parole) as we tended to lean on each other and didn't get too caught up with ghosts in the camp

(guys doing short-time who are just passing through).

About twenty years had passed and as the guys I had known for decades began to become parole eligible I began to get very antsy. It was hard to see guys I had known for decades suddenly have hope in their lives. I wanted them all to get out and to do well, but I was also frustrated because I knew that the brain science that was getting them relief also applied to me.

They said at the time of the Miller v. Alabama decision that the brain science applied to people up to 25 years old. I got arrested at 21 and that was the second group of people that the brain science applied to, those aged 18-21.

Eventually, I wrote to C.P.C.S. (Committee for Public Counsel Service) and asked them to screen my case to see if the Miller decision could apply to me, or if my lawyers had failed to litigate any claim. They assigned my case to a truly special and wonderful woman who would become my lawyer (Amy Belger). She found an issue in my case that did not exist in 1995.

I therefore had a shot at relief.

In 2013 the S.J.C. decided Commonwealth v. Marinho, 464 Mass. 115. For the first time the S.J.C. stated that there is a specific duty on the part of the defense counsel to advocate for a client through plea negotiations for a disposition that is materially better than what the client can receive at trial. Failure to do so amounts to deficient performance on the part of counsel. Marinho was decided in 2013, but I wouldn't learn about it until 2015 when my lawyer told me it was exactly on point for me.

I will deal with the Marinho issue in an upcoming chapter but for now it is sufficient for the reader to know that this gave me a legal issue I didn't have prior to the Marinho decision of 2013. I had enough standing with this issue to not only get my lawyer appointed but also to have the District Attorney's office offer to reduce my sentence from a first degree (life without parole) to a second degree (parole eligible after 15 years). Not only that, but the same District Attorney who prosecuted me was still alive and was WILLING TO COME INTO COURT AND

TESTIFY ON MY BEHALF ABOUT THIS ISSUE.

This is almost unprecedented that the D.A.'s office would offer to reduce, and that the prosecuting attorney would come into court to help.

Much as I tried not to get my hopes up too much, I couldn't help but do so (hope is a dangerous thing to a lifer because we do not control our own destiny). I began to have hope, to envision a future, to work on a realistic release plan and to line up job prospects and a support network. My dreams of flying returned with the idea of freedom. I was considering how I would live out my remaining years in such a different way than I had lived out my early years. I would center myself in my yoga imagining doing my routine on a mountain, on a beach or on a mesa overlooking a desert.

I was also hopeful that the brain science would be extended to that next group of 18 to 21-year-olds. I certainly knew that I had changed and no longer thought like a teen or acted like a teen. I knew that every fiber of my being was different than the one that was arrested at twenty-one.

I have spoken about several court cases which kept making progress a little bit at a time on the issue of juvenile offenders and life without parole, but the people we have not heard from yet are those tied to the brain science. I will now allow some of them to introduce the subject as they are so much more eloquent and knowledgeable about these issues than I am.

A study from the Massachusetts Department of Correction researched brain development in young males.

"The Influence of Brain Development Research on the Response to Young Adult Males 18 – 24 Years of Age in the Criminal Justice System" was written by Rhianna Kohl, PhD, Executive Director, and prepared by Susan McDonald, Senior Research Analyst, in the Office of Strategic Planning and Research: November 2018. The study describes the U.S. legal system's history in treating juvenile offenders, some younger than age ten, like adults and imposing the same penalties adults received.

In the late twentieth century, extensive research into the development and maturity of young brains has led to greater understanding of the juvenile behavior, with researchers concluding that people do not reach full mental maturity until their mid-twenties or beyond. Here is Dr. Kohl's assessment of those findings in terms of judicial proceedings and criminal cases that involve young people.

In recent years, this trend [treating juveniles as adults] has started to reverse with the return to a separate, more rehabilitative system that recognizes the special needs and immature status of young people. (2-3)

On February 5, 2018, the American Bar Association House of Delegates passed Resolution 111 revising their position with regards to young adults and the death penalty. "This resolution urges each death penalty jurisdiction to not execute or sentence to death anyone who was 21 years old or younger at the time of the offense" (American Bar Association, 2018). The decision to revise their position is based on "a growing medical consensus that key areas of the brain relevant to decision-making and judgment continue to develop into the early twenties. With this position has come a corresponding public understanding that our criminal justice system should also evolve in how it treats late adolescents (individuals aged 18 to 21 years old), ranging from their access to juvenile court alternatives to eligibility for the death penalty" (American Bar Association, 2018). The acknowledgement of the period of late adolescence and young adulthood as a time of continued brain growth and maturation and that this age group is resilient to change speaks to the need for different tactics to deal with this population in the criminal justice system.

The research shows that mental maturity continues through the mid-twenties (National Offender Management Service, 2015, August). Specialized courts, parole programs, correctional housing units and facilities have begun to appear throughout the United States with a focus on young adults between 18 and 23.

The study lists several legal cases involving teenagers and young adults convicted of capital crimes. As brain science continues to evolve, the courts are responding accordingly to apply age-appropriate sentences to younger offenders.

The Supreme Court has rendered numerous decisions over the past forty years that have shaped the way juvenile justice is practiced today, including decisions regarding the death penalty and life sentences for increasingly older juveniles. Although a decision has not yet been put forth allowing the same rights to offenders over the age of eighteen that are provided to juveniles under the age of eighteen in regard to capital and life sentences, the subject has been broached, and lower courts are beginning to rule in favor of extending protections to young adults over the age of eighteen. Continued advances in science and additional evidence regarding the development of young adult brains may influence future decisions.

The court decisions above show the progress of juvenile sentencing in regard to the most serious crimes and severe sentences. In these cases, "the court acknowledged that adolescents and adults are different in legally relevant ways" relying on "developmental science for confirmation of what 'any parent knows'", as justice Kennedy put it in his majority opinion in Roper (Steinberg, 2017). As this science continues to advance, more information will be forthcoming regarding the continuation of brain maturation into the early to mid-twenties, and this will add to the evolution of juvenile sentencing in the future (7) (download (mass.gov).

A 2019 study, "Teenage Brain Development: Its Impact on Criminal Activity and Trial Sentencing" by Gretchen M. Colon-Fuentes states that the brain continues to develop toward maturity between the ages of eleven and twenty-four, with many brains not developing the judgment areas fully until the late twenties or beyond. This supports previous and growing research that the brain's executive functions for decision making, risk management, and impulsivity develop later than sensory and motor skills:

Brain development, specifically the pre-frontal cortex, will not fully be developed until late twenties or even later, which is why "risk-taking, and impulsive behavior are more common among teens and young adults" (1067) (88RevJurUPR1062 (uprrp.edu).

Important research continues in the study of youthful brain development, with implications not only evolving in the area of criminal justice but also in higher education and socialization skills. Improved understanding of these areas and their interrelatedness may have a bearing on the future of juvenile court sentences.

Chapter 8

Whitepaper

The whitepaper on the topic of juvenile crimes and sentencing offers detailed research. Since it is almost sixty pages long, I believe most readers will not want to invest that deeply in the subject. I have included here the executive summary and the introduction, which distills the document into a more manageable nine pages.

I appreciate the work being done and claim none of it as my own.

Please see attached hereto by permission of the authors: Center for Law, Brain 8 Behavior at Massachusetts General Hospital (2022): White Paper on the science of late adolescence, A Guide for Judges, Attorneys and Policymakers (January 27, 2022) (White Paper on the Science of Late Adolescence: A Guide for Judges, Attorneys, and Policy Makers Center for Law, Brain & Behavior (harvard.edu)

Executive Summary

The United States Supreme Court decision in Jones v. Mississippi (2021)[1] almost certainly signals the end of further expansion at this time by SCOTUS of Eighth Amendment protections to juveniles.[2] Jones v. Mississippi held that a sentencing court need not make a specific finding that a youth is "permanently incorrigible" or even articulate a specific Miller v. Alabama rationale for a sentencing decision guided by factors provided in Miller v. Alabama.[3] It was enough that the sentencing judge understood that he or she had discretion to consider the Miller factors and made an individualized sentencing decision—a very low bar.[4]

In addition, the legal framework established by the Roper-Graham-Miller-Montgomery line of SCOTUS cases in barring execution for juvenile capital offenses.[5] Life Without Parole (JLWOP) for juvenile non-homicide cases,[6] and mandatory LWOP for juvenile homicide cases[7] has been incorporated to varying degrees into state statutes and case law and offers at least the possibility for a more robust application of Miller. The Miller approach also remains viable for pursuing expansion of those categorical protections to age 18 and beyond, and perhaps for raising the age of full criminal culpability.

The Miller framework's focus on "transient immaturity" also offers a way of asserting protections for young offenders in individual cases.[8] Arguably, shifting the focus from "permanent incorrigibility" (which cannot be predicted in a scientifically reliable manner) to "transient immaturity" (which is already established by robust developmental research and neuroscience) may provide opportunities for counsel and courts at trial/sentencing phases and upon appellate review. It may also encourage prosecutors to consider research-based diversion and community-based intervention programs as alternatives to traditional charging decisions and sentencing recommendations.

Similarly, the explicit reliance in these SCOTUS cases upon developmental neuroscience and behavioral science offers models for using science to advance broad evidence-based law and policy reforms regarding juveniles and emerging young adults. This White Paper reports the latest developmental and brain science to inform judges, attorneys, and policy makers about critical research developments.[9] This White Paper is intended to facilitate science-informed decision-making and application of updated research findings in law and public policy bearing upon adolescence and criminal proceedings.

1. Jones v. Mississippi, 141 S. Ct. 1307 (2021).
2. For purposes of this White Paper, the following terms are used to describe young people of different ages: (a) juveniles: broadly, persons between 13—17; (b) early adolescents: persons ages 10—13; (c) middle adolescents: persons ages 14—17; (d) late adolescents: persons ages 18—21; and (e) young adults: persons ages 22—25.

3 Jones, 141 S. Ct. at 1311.

4. Id.
5. Roper v. Simmons, 543 U.S. 551 (2005).

6. Graham v. Florida, 560 U.S. 48 (2010).
7. Miller v. Alabama, 567 U.S. 460 (2012); Montgomery v. Louisiana, 577 U.S. 190, 211 (2016) (extending Miller retroactively).
8. Miller, 567 U.S. at 479.

In the landmark case Miller v. Alabama (2012), the United States Supreme Court eliminated mandatory life-without-parole sentences for murders committed by youth under age 18. [10] This decision was informed by an evolving understanding of adolescent brain development and behavioral research. Since then, scientific research has emerged which reinforces the reasoning of the Miller decision and, if its implications are accepted, extends much of the science that resonated with the Miller court to late adolescents (ages 18—21).

Maturation of brain structure, brain function, and brain connectivity continues throughout the early twenties. This ongoing brain development has profound implications for decision-making, self-control and emotional processing. For example, new neuroscience research reveals that during emotionally charged situations, late adolescents (ages 18—21) respond more like younger adolescents (ages 13—17) than like young adults (ages 22—25) due to differences in brain maturation. [12]

Compared to young adults above age 21, late adolescents (ages 18—21) also take more risks and engage in more sensation-seeking behavior. [13] Due to differences in brain development, late adolescents are more likely than young adults to respond to immediate outcomes and are less likely to delay gratification. [14] The presence of peers can intensify these behaviors, and the brains of late adolescents are more responsive to peer involvement than those of young adults. [15] Late adolescents are also more easily swayed by adult influence and coercion than their adult counterparts. [16] These developmental differences in behavior have direct implications for legal decision-making, including waiving Miranda rights, susceptibility to false confessions, and making ill-advised trial decisions (e.g., plea decisions).

9. See Appendix A for a foundational review of the science. For an extensive review of brain and socio-behavioral research and its policy implications, see also National Academies of Sciences, Engineering, and Medicine. The Promise of Adolescence: Realizing Opportunity for All Youth. (2019), https://doi.org/10.17226/25388; Institute of Medicine and National Research Council, Investing in the Health and

Well-Being of Young Adults (2015), https://doi.org/10.17226/18869.
10 Miller, 567 U.S. at 480.

11. Leah Somerville, Searching for Signatures of Brain Maturity: What Are We Searching For? 92 Neuron 1 164, 1 164-67 (2016).
12. Alexandra O. Cohen et al., When Is an Adolescent an Adult? Assessing Cognitive Control in Emotional and Non-emotional Contexts, 27 Psych. Sci. 549 (2016); Marc D. Rudolph et al., At Risk of Being Risky: The Relationship Between "Brain Age" Under Emotional States and Risk Preference, 24 Developmental Cognitive. Neuroscience-, 93, 93—106 (2017); B. J. Casey et al, Development of the Emotional Brain, 29 Neuroscience Letters 693 (2019).
13. Laurence Steinberg, Adolescent Brain Science and Juvenile Justice Policymaking, 23 Psych., Pub. Policy, & L 410 (2017).
14. Michelle Achterberg et al, Fronto-striatal White Matter Integrity Predicts Development of Delay of Gratification: A Longitudinal Study, 36 J. Neuroscience. 1954 (2016); Samuel Hawes et al, Modulation of Reward-Related Neural Activation on Sensation Seeking Across Development, 147 Neuroimage 763 (2017).
15. Dustin Albert, Jason Chein & Laurence Steinberg, The Teenage Brain: Peer Influences on Adolescent Decision-Making, 22 Current Directions Psych. Sci. 114 (2013); Ashley Smith et al, Age Differences in the Impact of Peers on Adolescents' and Adults' Neural Response to Reward, 11 Developmental Cognitive Neuroscience 75 (2015).
16. Hayley Cleary, Applying the Lessons of Developmental Psychology to the Study of Juvenile Interrogations: New Directions for Research, Policy, and Practice, 23 Psych., Pub. Policy, & L, 118, 118—130 (2017).

Adversity, racism, and poverty also have a profound impact on health, quality of life, and criminal justice involvement. [17] As discussed below, adolescents who have experienced adversity, racism, and poverty are significantly overrepresented in juvenile and criminal justice systems. However, while these experiences pose developmental challenges, they do not dictate fate, as late adolescents are also remarkably resilient, and their developing brains are poised for positive learning through interventions and rehabilitation. [18]

For late adolescents engaged in criminal behavior, research consistently indicates that most will not continue to offend and become adult repeat offenders through their twenties, thirties, and beyond. [19] This has significant implications for both policy and the legal system. For example, this high rate of desistance from even serious or persistent adolescents offending as youth move into their early to mid-twenties renders it impossible to reliably predict, based on current science, which individual youth will continue to offend into adulthood, and which will desist as they mature. There is certainly no basis in science to reliably determine that an individual youth at the time of sentencing in adolescence is incapable of rehabilitation (or even unlikely to achieve it) over the course of a lifetime.

While Jones v. Mississippi (2021) held that a sentencing court need not make a formal finding of "permanent incorrigibility" in considering a JLWOP sentence,[20] the Miller factors remain applicable and key to articulating the "transient" nature of adolescence generally and applying those factors in the individual case before the court. Science cannot divine which "rare" adolescent may be "permanently incorrigible," but it can identify the characteristically "transient characteristics" of adolescence.

One inherent challenge to incorporating science into litigation and decision-making lies in the application of research developed in studies on groups of subjects to the circumstances, conduct, and developmental trajectories of individual persons before the court. This is sometimes referred to as the "Group to Individual" conundrum. For example, developmental brain science can provide "on average" group-level descriptions of brain development and maturation which can be supplemented by consideration of the specific individual characteristics at issue in the legal context. This, of course, is a challenge that is familiar in the practice of medicine, where physicians must apply research based upon groups to diagnose and treat individuals.

In cases involving adolescents and late adolescents, research applied in individual cases must be derived from studies in multiple domains including neuroscience, social determinants of misconduct, peer affiliations and social networks, developmental trajectories, and individual characteristics (e.g., cognitive capacities, physical maturation, emotional characteristics, learning style, family dynamics).

17. Scott Lorch & Elizabeth Enlow, The Role of Social Determinants in Explaining Racial/Ethnic Disparities in Perinatal Outcomes 79 Pediatric Research. 141 (2016).

18. B.J Casey et al, Making the Sentencing Case: Psychological and Neuroscientific Evidence for Expanding the Age of Youthful Offenders, 5 Ann. Rev. Criminology (forthcoming 2022).
19. Off. Juv. Just. Delinq- Prot., Law Enforcement & Juvenile Crime: Arrests by Offense, Age, and Gender, U.S- Dept. Just. (Oct. 21, 2019), https://www.ojjdp.gov/ojstatbb/crime/ucr.asp?table_in=1 [https://perma.cc/T6H7-3LWX].
20. Jones v. Mississippi, 141 S. Ct. 1307, 1309 (2021).

This guide is intended to support attorneys and judges in familiarizing themselves with the contours of the relevant science and how it can be applied to individual cases. A working knowledge of developmental and brain science allows attorneys and judges to make best use of what a juvenile defendant's life course, circumstances of an alleged offense, and expert evaluations and opinions can tell them to assist in understanding a defendant.[21] For attorneys, this facilitates preparing a case, educating the legal finder of fact, and making optimal use of expert testimony. For judges, this facilitates science-informed decision-making at all trial and appellate phases of a case involving a juvenile or young adult.[22]

The goal is to position each individual young defendant within a developmental trajectory comprised of biological, psychological, and social domains. A significant majority of cases willultimately reflect "transitory immaturity," a feature of adolescence which will resolve as adolescents mature, resulting in desistance from criminal misconduct. Science-informed decision-making and evidence-based interventions can guide rehabilitation and reduce recidivism (thereby improving community safety) while avoiding or minimizing the negative impact of common responses (such as overuse of detention and incarceration) that can inadvertently compromise positive youth development and increase recidivism.

A better understanding of late adolescent brain and behavioral development can transform how the legal system and policy makers respond to late adolescents who offend. By educating decision-makers and advocates, this White Paper informs the criminal justice system and policy makers through providing an updated research perspective on late adolescence and supporting public safety by reducing recidivism through developmentally aligned accountability and empirically-based processes and interventions.

21. Readers conducting forensic evaluations or using these evaluations in legal proceedings can find guidance in generating or relying upon them from sources including Antoinette Kavanaugh & Thomas Grisso, Evaluations for Sentencing of Juveniles in Criminal Court (2020).
22. For a review of aspects of "developmental evidence" and application of the Miller factors, see Thomas Grisso & Antoinette Kavanaugh, Prospect& for Developmental Evidence in Juvenile Sentencing Based on Miller v. Alabama, 22 Psych. Pub. Policy & L. 235, 235—249 (2016); See also Thomas Grisso, Three Opportunities for the Future of Juvenile Forensic Assessment, 46 Crim. Just. & Behav. 1671 (2019), https•.//doi.org/10.1177/0093854819883671

Juveniles	Ages 13-17
Early Adolescence	Ages 10-13
Middle Adolescence	Ages 14—17
Late Adolescence	Ages 18-21
Young Adults	Ages 22-25

Age Ranges Defined for Purposes of this White Paper

Introduction

In a series of landmark decisions starting in 2005, the United States Supreme Court ruled that no one can be put to death,[23] receive a sentence of life without parole for a non-homicide offense, [24] or receive a sentence of mandatory life without parole for an offense committed prior to age 18.[25].

In drawing the line at age 18, the Supreme Court continued a tradition of raising the age at which Eighth Amendment protections against cruel and unusual punishment are applied. As Justice Stevens recognized in his concurring opinion in Roper v. Simmons, the holding reaffirmed the principle that "evolving standards of decency have driven [the Court's] construction of this critically important part of the Bill of Rights," and recognized that "if the meaning of that amendment had been frozen when it was originally drafted, it would impose no impediment to the execution of 7-year-old children today. "[26]

Jones v. Mississippi (2021) held that the requirements of Miller v. Alabama (2012) are satisfied if a juvenile's sentence of life without parole (JWOP) is imposed after an individualized hearing. Notably, the Jones majority did not reinforce the Miller court's view that this sentence should be "uncommon" and reserved for the "rare" youth deemed "permanently incorrigible." Indeed, the Jones decision held that a sentencing judge need not make a specific finding that a juvenile is "permanently incorrigible" or even make formal findings of fact in support of a discretionary sentencing decision. However, SCOTUS did not explicitly strike down the Miller factor framework, acknowledged that states may set their own standards and protections more stringently than the Jones approach[27] (which many states have), and left undisturbed the concept of the "transient immaturity" of youth reflected in decisions from Roper (2005) through Montgomery v. Louisiana (2016). [28]

23. Roper v. Simmons, 543 U.S. 551 (2005).
24. Graham v. Florida, 560 U.S. 48 (2010).
25. Miller v. Alabama, 567 U.S. 460 (2012).
26. Roper, 543 U.S. at 1205.
27. Jones v. Mississippi, 141 S. Ct. 1307, 1322 (2021).
28. Montgomery v. Louisiana, 136 S. Ct. 718 (2016)

The Jones court abandoned any consideration of "evolving standards of decency" that might lead to the abolition of JLWOP outright, although case law and statutes in many states since Miller have taken that step. Other states have established minimum sentences[29] to be served before juvenile homicide offenders are afforded the requirement set by the Miller court for a "meaningful" opportunity to demonstrate that they have achieved rehabilitation.

The Jones court paid scant attention to the scientific foundations of the Roper through

Montgomery line of cases. By contrast, prior to the dilution by Jones of protections afforded to juvenile offenders, SCOTUS Eighth Amendment rulings about sentencing youthful offenders had drawn heavily from advances in social sciences and neurodevelopmental research. [30] The court cited scientific publications when it ruled that the Eighth Amendment prohibits the death penalty for those under age 18 at the time of their capital offense;[31] prohibits life without the possibility of parole (LWOP) for non-homicide offenders under age 18 at the time of their offense; [32] and prohibits mandatory life imprisonment without parole for those under age 18 at the time of the offense, even for homicide offenses.[33]

From those scientific studies it cited, the court reached the conclusion that youth are less morally culpable, more susceptible to peer pressure, and more amenable to positive change. .Indeed, SCOTUS had absolutely barred for juveniles as a class both execution and life without possibility of parole for non-homicide offenses, reflecting a strong "children are different" approach to Eighth Amendment constitutional doctrine.

The Miller majority stepped back from this categorical "children are different" approach when it barred mandatory LWOP but permitted it for a presumably very small number of "permanently incorrigible" youth based on a judge's discretion following an individualized sentencing hearing. In doing so, however, the Miller court reaffirmed the law's recognition that "relevance of youth as a mitigating factor derives from the fact that the signature qualities of youth are transient; as individuals mature, the impetuousness and recklessness which may dominate in younger years can subside." 34

Although the Jones majority did not focus upon the "transient immaturity" of youth, legislative and case law developments among the states implementing Miller suggest the concept of ."transient immaturity" may be central to incorporating into litigation and policy advocacy the .continuing developments in science. While there is no scientifically reliable basis to predict that a youthful offender is "permanently incorrigible," there is a robust scientific basis, as describedin this Guide, to identify the "transient immaturity" of youth and emerging young adults and the normal process of self-desistence from criminal misconduct that occurs with maturation. The Miller factors still serve as a framework for organizing and explaining. This research and as a means for accounting for the hallmarks of youthful immaturity, the circumstances of their offenses, and their greater prospects for self-desistence with maturation alone or with the support of empirically based interventions.

29. Litigation continues to clarify at what point a lengthy minimum mandatory sentence for a juvenile offender violates the Miller requirement there be afforded a "meaningful" opportunity to demonstrate achievement of rehabilitation. The disparity among states of minimum mandatory terms to be served range from less than two decades to four or more decades, resulting in a problematic "justice by geography" situation where sentenced youthful offenders may serve sentences for the same offenses that differ by decades before a putatively "meaningful" case review.
30. See, e.g., Miller, 567 IJ.S. at 471 (noting relevance of studies in American Psychologist and other journals for the reasoning in Roper and Graham).
31. Roper v. Simmons, 543 U.S. 551 (2005).
32. Graham v. Horida, 560 U.S. 48 (2010). Graham held that states must provide "meaningful opportunity to obtain release based on demonstrated maturity and rehabilitation." Id. at 75.
33. Miller 567 U.S. at 460.
34. [d. at 1 195—96 (Internal citations omitted).

This White Paper reviews recent scientific research establishing that these same "signature qualities of youth" extend into the period of late adolescence (ages 18-21). Since the Supreme Court decided Miller v. Alabama in 2012, more than one hundred new publications have explored the brain's development throughout late adolescence. Over 1,000 legal cases have referenced the same or similar neuroscience to that discussed in Miller, with many citing newer scientific articles as well. [35] Roughly half of these cases concerned individuals who were 18 years old or older at the time of the offenses for which they were charged.

In addition to their implications for legal challenges, the scientific findings reported in this White Paper are relevant for criminal justice policy. Late adolescents (ages 18-21) and young adults (ages 22—25) make up approximately 10-12% of the U.S. population, [36] yet this age group accounts for 23% of all arrests. [37] Late adolescents also make up 20% of incarcerated persons. [38] Youth of color are disproportionately represented, [39] as half of incarcerated 1 8—24-year-olds are people of color. 40 Additionally, many of these incarcerated late adolescents and young adults face long prison sentences. Almost 40% of the individuals serving the longest prison sentences in the United States were incarcerated before age 25, and 56% of those serving the longest sentences are black. [41]

35. Francis X. Shen, et al., Justice for Emerging Adults after Jones: The Rapidly Developing Use of Neuroscience to Extend Eighth Amendment Miller Protections to Defendants Ages 18 and Older, 97 N.Y.U. L. Rev. Online (forthcoming 2022) (examining how the science proffered in Miller has been cited in subsequent cases).
36. Population estimates vary depending upon demographic data sources and years the samples were derived. See Just. Policy Inst., Improving Approaches to Serving Young Adults in the Justice System 3 (2016) (9.9% of U.S. population); see also Annie E. Casey foundation, Kids Count Data Center https://datacenter.kidscount.org/ (last visited April 17, 2021) (similar).

Alternatively, one could calculate this percentage by combining population data sources: for example, the U.S. Census Bureau projected a total U.S. population of 326,971,407 on January 1, 2018. U.S. Census Bur., Census Bureau Projects U.S. and Wodd Populations (Dec. 28, 2017), https://www.census.gov/newsroom/press-releases/2017/new-years-2018.html[https://perma.cc/8MKP-FUHU]. -The Center for Education Statistics estimated a population of 30,600,000 18 to 24-year-olds for the same date. National Center For Ed. Statistics, Indicator 1: Population Distribution (Feb. 2019), https://nces.ed.gov/programs/ raceindicatorsnndicator_ RAA.asp [https://perma.cc/9XZQ-YRY9] (last visited Dec. 12, 2020). 30,600,000 divided by 326,971,407 equals about 9.36%.

37. See Office of Juvenile Justice and Delinquency Prevention, estimated number of arrests by offense and age group, U.S. Dep't of Justice (201 g), https://www.ojjdp.gov/ojstatbb/crime/ucr.asp?table_in=l [https://perma.cc/T6H7—3LWXl (last visited April 18, 2021). To calculate the percentage of offenses committed by those between 18 and 24 for each year between 2015 to 2019, add total offenses for the 18 to 20 age group and the total offenses for the 21 to 24 age group, then divide that total by the total number of offenses for all ages. Results

are (rounded to the hundredths place): 19.88% for 2019, 21.69% for 201 8, 23.15% for 2017, 24.62% for 2016, and 25.67% for 2015. Averages for the past five years of data were derived by adding these five percentages together and then dividing by 5 to get 23.002%. A five-year annual average was used to reflect continuity. Worth noting, however, is the declining trend: Each year from 2015 to 2019, the percentage of crimes committed by those between 18 and 24 decreased. Affirmatively put, in 2019, 19.88% of all arrests in the U.S. were for offenses committed by individuals from 18 to 24 years old, a percentage slightly less than in the previous four years. This arrest data was crosschecked with FBI data available for 2016 (last available year) which also resulted in an arrest rate calculation of 24.62%. See Crim. Just. Servs. Div., 2016 Crime in the United States, Fed. Bur. Investigation (2016), https://ucr.fbi.gov/crime-in-the-U.S./2016/crime-in-the-u.s.-2016/tables/table-20 [https://perma.cc/NWQ2-HYGW] (last visited Dec. 12, 2020).

38. Just. Policy Inst., Improving Approaches to Serving Young Adults in the Justice System 1 (2016), http://www.justicepolicy.org/uploads/justicepolicy/documentsopi_report_summary_improving_approaches_to_serving_young_adults_in_the_justice_sys-tem.pdf [https://perma.cc/NPU6-YUYRl (last visited Apr. 18, 2021).
39. Id. at 2 ("The data show ... that young adults of color are disproportionately impacted by the justice system."). 40 year-olds are people of color.[40] Additionally, many of these incarcerated late adolescents and young adults face long sentences. Almost 40% of the individuals serving the longest prison sentences in the United States were incarcerated before age 255 and 56% of those serving the longest sentences are black.[41]

Research in neuroscience, psychology, and law have contributed to an evolving understanding of both behavioral and brain development during adolescence. This contemporary research has direct implications for juvenile justice policy and practice.[42] This White Paper assembles and synthesizes both foundational and recent scientific developments to provide an updated overview of the science of late adolescence.

Foundational background information summarizing contemporary research on adolescent brain development is presented in Appendix A for readers who would benefit from a primer or refresher on the basic neuroscience.[43] This paper presents a synthesis of the brain and behavioral science most relevant for understanding legal and policy implications of these areas of research. The science is organized by the distinguishing characteristics of youth identified as critical factors by SCOTUS in Miller and is subsequently reflected, further developed, or limited.

Post-Miller activity involving juvenile defendants[44] and defendants ages 18 and older largely reflects actions taken by state courts and legislatures.[45] We anticipate that, particularly following the Jones decision in Spring 2021, most legal and legislative activity in this area will continue to occur at the state rather than federal level. The Miller factors have made their way into state case law and policy debates and so continue to be relevant. The Miller factors that serve as the organizing factors for the science presented in this paper are: immaturity, impetuosity, and risk-taking. The "hallmark features" of adolescence include "immaturity, impetuosity, and a failure to appreciate risks and consequences."

40. Id at 1.
41. Urban Inst., A Matter of Time: The Causes and Consequences of Rising Time Served in America's Prisons (2017), https://apps.urban.org/featuresnong-prison-tems/demographics.htmt [https://pema.cc/CQ6V-QP3L] Oast visited Apr. 18, 2021).
42. B.J. Casey et al, Healthy Development as a Human Right Insights from Developmental Neuroscience for Youth Justice, 16 Ann. Rev. L & Soc- Sci- 9.1 (2020); B.J. Casey et al, Making the Sentencing Case: Psychological and Neuroscientific Evidence for Expanding the Age of Youthful Offenders, 5 Ann. Rev. Criminology (forthcoming 2022); Leark, R. A. (2021). An Introduction to the Special Issue on the Death Penalty Among Teen-Aged Offenders. 7 J. Pediatric Neuropsych. 1—2 (2021).
43. The authors acknowledge that contemporary neuroscience increasingly focuses upon neural circuit connections and extraordinarily complex interactions among brain regions rather than merely attribution of functions to "lobes" or other specific brain areas. However,

the published research often references structure and function of specific brain areas and so the reporting of brain research will often make references to specific brain areas.

44. By 2020, courts or legislatures in at least 19 states had barred life without parole for juvenile defendants. See, e.g., Diatchenko v. Dist. Atty for Suffolk Dist., 1 N.E.3d 270 (Mass. 2013); State v. Bassett, 428 P.3d 343 (Wash. 2018). For a review of post-Miller actions by state courts and legislatures, see Gina Kim, State-by-State Abolition of Juvenile Life without Parole Sentences in the United States since Miller v. Alabama (2012), (2019) (Ph.D. dissertation, Columbia University; available through Academic Commons, Columbia University Libraries).
45. For a review of post-Miller use of neuroscience in litigation involving late adolescents, see Francis Shen et al, Justice for Emerging Adults after Jones: The Rapidly Developing Use of Neuroscience to Extend Eighth Amendment Miller Protections to Defendants Ages 18 and Older, 97 N.Y.U. LRev. Online (forthcoming 2021).

Peer involvement / influence "[T]he family and home environment that surrounds him—and from which he cannot usually extricate himself—no matter how brutal or dysfunctional the circumstances of the homicide offense, including the extent of his participation in the conduct and the way familial and peer pressures may have affected him."

Understanding Legal Proceedings Deficits in legal understandings were described as: "the incompetencies associated with youth" including an "inability to deal with police officers or prosecutors (including on a plea agreement)" and "incapacity to assist his own attorneys."

Greater Potential for Rehabilitation. The greater potential of adolescents for rehabilitation was first recognized in Roper. This greater potential for positive change and the absence of a scientific basis to reliably identify that "rare" youth whose "permanent incorrigibility" warrants LWOP continue to present a challenge to sentencing courts.

Jones v. Mississippi (2021) held that a separate finding of "permanent incorrigibility" is not required in a discretionary sentencing to LWOP.[46] However, opportunities to inform sentencing procedures and decisions with the science presented in this White Paper remain due to: (a) the long-standing recognition of the "transient immaturity of youth" resulting in diminished culpability; (b) the common self-desistance from misconduct as youth mature; and, (c) law requiring analysis using the so-called Miller factors in these cases. The science is also relevant to adolescents older than the current "bright line" of age 18 for criminal culpability.

Especially in state cases, there are opportunities to inform legislatures, sentencing procedures, and individual case sentencing decisions with the science presented in this White Paper, particularly in state proceedings. Each of these distinguishing characteristics are discussed below for middle to late adolescents in light of broadly accepted leading research.

Readers who want further description of foundational neuroscience are directed to Appendix A at page 47 for a summary.

46. Jones v. Mississippi, 141 S. Ct. 1307, 1311 (2021).

Chapter 9

Progress

As previously discussed, when I arrived at Norfolk, I began learning Spanish. I consider this an unofficial program because it is not offered by the D. O. C. as part of a curriculum, and there are no certificates for completion. It is simply a group of men getting together to study and do something goal directed. Whether the D. O. C. recognizes it or not, language study is nevertheless a program that I participated in for years. I began as an inept student with no capacity for the language and ended with me teaching others the basics of Spanish grammar. Due to the Covid pandemic, we shut down for two years but recently resumed the class and there is still a great deal of intertest in it. The faces may have changes, but the people are still wanting to learn, to grow, and to better themselves.

Toastmasters

In 2011, 1 began to participate in the Toastmasters speech club. We had a charter to exist as a Toastmasters International branch, and we operated as the Phoenix Club. I do not know if the Club continues to exist since Covid lockdown, but I hope it does, as men have gained from that program in many ways.

Toastmasters is a club where people learn public speaking skills. In 2011, I was looking for something to keep me occupied. I had heard of Toastmasters before but didn't know much about the organization, so I decided to check it out as I had been shy and introverted all my life. It was not that I didn't have things to say, it was just that I had zero .confidence for speaking up in groups. That fear of rejection gets set early in life and may take a lifetime to overcome. By this point, I was no longer that scared child and wanted to speak to others about worthwhile topics.

During the previous twenty years I had been emerging from my cocoon of reserve and had been gaining confidence each year with exposure to principles of mindfulness, such as Buddhism and yoga. I learned to relax and use meditation to live in the moment. In doing that, I was better able to get on with what I was trying to do.

When I went to that first Toastmasters meeting, there was a diverse crowd, and they were all smiling and happy. I didn't completely trust "happy" after so many years in the max, but I thought it was better than the alternative. Still, I was not used to people being welcoming. Toastmasters had a greeter at the door, which was different. As I approached the greeter, I felt a good vibe coming from the participants in the room. I had learned how to assess negative energy quickly from all those years in the max, but this was different. The room was filled with positive energy, which was a very welcome change. Since becoming more mindful, I was beginning to draw more positive energy in my direction. As the old saying goes, "You get what you give."

I sat quietly as I watched the presentations. The Toastmaster introduced the role players, the timer table topics master, and the speakers. They asked those who were new to stand and introduce themselves. I stood up and said my name, feeling exposed. After introductions, we sat through the meeting and listened to the speakers. I liked the way they presented topics; it was good to hear people talk about things other than prison. That was uplifting. I got to know the guys in that session, and we had a good crew as well as fantastic speakers.

I watched that first meeting with interest and liked when table topics were introduced. For readers who do not know, table topics are questions posed to people in the audience and require that you give a response of thirty seconds or one minute. What is tricky is that they can be based on any subject whatsoever. The idea is to get you to think on your feet and to respond without thinking too long on a subject. Sometimes the results are comical because the questions can be bizarre, or the guy responding to the question may draw a complete blank and struggle to answer. I didn't know then how good our group was. We had many guys in the camp, and all seemed to want to do something positive. Most of our guys were also taking classes from Boston University, which offered a degree program back then. Yes, we appealed to the intellectual, nerdy types who were trying to keep their minds occupied with something positive, but we also had a huge group who were participating in other programs as well. Those who were doing multiple programs were not the ones interested in getting high. We had such a good group of speakers to come out of Toastmasters that I felt proud to be part of it. I liked the program's format and structure.

I went on to become more involved and earned the Competent Communicator certificate in 2012, the Advanced Communicator bronze in 2013, the Advanced Communicator silver in 2014, and the Advanced Communicator gold in 2015. On the leadership track I earned the Competent Leader award in 2012 and the Advanced Leader bronze in 2015. I also earned numerous certificates for debates, for participating in a contest, and for judging a contest. Then in 2014-2015, I became President of the Club. It was around this time that I wrote to C. P.C. S. (Committee for Public Counsel Services) to try and get a lawyer to represent me. I would be assigned a lawyer, but now I had new priorities. Due to these priorities I needed to bail out of Toastmasters and put my focus on programs.

I had always done some programs that I thought would help me: college courses, welding, creative writing, Toastmaster's, and even learned a second language. I had not done any of the deep introspective soul-searching work on why I went so wrong in life. I was ready to do that trauma work now.

I didn't think I would fit in because I couldn't claim poverty, sexual abuse, or a crackhead mother as reasons for ending up in prison. I saw there was more reason to participate in the trauma work than not. I would eventually do considerable work on early childhood trauma and come to a much better understanding of my childhood issues.

What I didn't anticipate was that I would enjoy the programs and find that I liked going deep into trauma and soul healing. When I got involved with programs of this type, I started with an open mind and a good attitude, determined to get what I could out of them. I knew even before the first program that we were going to be examining old emotional wounds. Down deep, I was aware that I was sitting on issues that needed work, and I was looking forward to it.

Restorative Justice

One of the most popular and respected groups in Norfolk is Restorative Justice. The concept springs from a Native American principle that if you harm an individual, you hurt the community. The community is considered a holistic healing place. The idea is that we are all part of the same community, and if you hurt one member, you hurt all. I have not been on the Board of Restorative Justice, but I have been a participant in some of their functions. While no expert, I can share my experience. Restorative Justice usually begins with the families who have lost children to murder. In many ways it is for and about them, but that doesn't tell the whole story. People may come who are not the families of murder victims. They might have been robbed, raped, or otherwise traumatized by members of the community.

These families come into prison with volunteers who are on board with the Restorative Justice model of healing. Participants often include senators, legislators, district attorneys, policy makers, judges, law enforcement, social workers, and other community employees or supporters.

You may think that having people from historically opposite sides of the criminal justice system would be very awkward, but you would be mistaken. It is the beginning of dialogue between people coming from divergent places.

When these victims and survivors arrive with their guests, they are escorted to the auditorium where all the prisoners who have signed up on the roster are waiting. The day will usually begin with these victims and survivors making a statement about how murder has affected them and their families, which is always compelling. Many men in the audience are incarcerated for murder, and this may be their first interaction with someone who has been affected by that crime.

Following this portion of the program, there might be a gathering where a subject is broached, and members of the audience can respond. Then we are organized into smaller groups called healing circles. These circles become intense, personal, and emotional as people speak their truth. From my experience, to sit across from a mother who has lost a child to murder and listen to her pain is a huge awakening. Knowing that you have caused that same pain in someone else's life is a heartbreaking and gut-wrenching experience. Restorative Justice gives participants the opportunity to understand the devastating effects that crime and violence have on the people involved on both sides.

In prison, we have learned to compartmentalize our feelings, traumas, shame, guilt, and degradation into small boxes that we store away so that we don't become overwhelmed by them (which is easy to do). Restorative Justice is one of the places where we pull open those drawers and look at the contents. This is also the concept of most other prison groups. The families hear our stories and come to know how we ended up in prison for committing these crimes. Policy makers come in and see what is going on, and some stay and do their own work in circles. It is quite a thing seeing state or federal prosecutors having honest discussions on critical issues that can tear a community apart but also launch the healing process.

Not all victims and survivors are at a place of forgiveness and healing, and not all prisoners are fully ready to own their crimes. But all respect why we are there and what we are trying to do. These people are entitled to whatever they are feeling. What it begins to do is let us see each other as human beings who share in the desire for safety, love, family, happiness, and prosperity - to have a life and a future.

This is just one aspect of Restorative Justice during the weekend retreat. Subsequently, other activities become available. Men can sign up for an eight-week reading group that introduces more issues of consideration for those who participated in the weekend retreats. After that is a "VOGUE" group (Victim, Offender, Education Group) that lasts for thirty-two weeks. Men who have participated in the weekend retreat and the reading group are eligible to attend this branch of the program. In this group, the entire Restorative Justice crew might work more in depth with the men who attend and get to know them on a personal basis. These men work with all kinds of people from the Restorative Justice and criminal justice communities.

Restorative Justice Yoga is an offshoot program in which I participated. It is a twenty-week course that incorporates yoga, mindfulness, trauma work, and meditation. The Asanas poses are what most people think of as classical yoga, but this only addresses the body. These are one limb of yoga on the eight-limb path. Yoga also deals with mind and spirit, in restorative justice we also deal with those aspects. In simple terms, we are doing healing work on the spirit and mind instead of just focusing on the body. I have recently completed a 10-week Facilitator's Training for this yoga class and will be in the running to be one of the Facilitators for the next 20-week class.

Emotional Awareness

Norfolk Prison was providing two courses about emotional awareness: Basic Emotional Awareness and Advanced Emotional Awareness. A person could not take the second without completing the first. Emotional Awareness provides participants an opportunity to look more deeply at their early history to understand the nature of their trauma and the impact it has had on their lives. Each class is thirteen weeks, and every person is expected to share and participate.

Participants were asked to write a first chapter of their autobiographies for the basic class as a starting point with a description of their childhood. This was read in front of the entire class. Each person shared as the others listened. Through this process the classmates began to see commonalities in all of us. They started to feel compassion for each other. At that point, the program's external volunteer would usually question participants about their experiences, ask for clarification, and acknowledge the trauma they had experienced as young children. The program leader demonstrated empathic listening. The rest of the class followed suit and continued to ask questions.

During this time handouts were given that identify risk factors for adolescent violent behavior. Understanding the circumstances in their childhood that predisposed them to antisocial behavior provided a new perspective. Listening with compassion to others as they share allowed everyone to view their own lives with greater compassion. Each week someone would share their autobiography. The basic concepts of the book *Houses of Healing* by Robin Casarjian are these: The Core Self, The Inner Child, The Five Feelings - Mad, Sad, Glad, Afraid, Ashamed, there is a focus on "mad and ashamed." The program leader volunteer would then suggest the men go deeper into their stories, asking questions of each participant based on what has been shared.

The next section deals with the question of violence and crime. As James Gilligan states in his book, *Violence*, all violence "is an attempt to replace shame with self-esteem." We get into talking about this point and what it means to feel shame or to be ashamed. The men are expected to bring in a detailed account of their crime. This would not be shared openly in class. The program leader would read these accounts privately to gain insight into what factors may have triggered people in their criminal behavior, and he or she would give insight into what may trigger them in their daily lives.

The next phase of this class gets into what is trauma, and what are triggers. We define trauma as psychological, physical, sexual, neglect, abandonment, mental illness, and not having ones needs met. We see triggers as indications of unhealed trauma, and we discuss the need to speak about these things.

That section is followed by the phase that deals with masks and sub-personalities. Using the book *Houses of Healing*, sub-personalities are defined as the behaviors that people exhibit when their basic needs for emotional and physical safety are not met in childhood. We begin to talk about the ways we acted out to protect ourselves. At one point in our childhoods, we may have needed to function as the "tough guy," "the cool kid," "the rebel," "the lover," "the comedian," and other personas to protect ourselves. However, these masks seldom help us as adults, and to get rid of them, we need to first acknowledge and then deal with them. We peel back each layer of the onion to get at what is lying beneath.

Societal devaluation, disruption of primary community, dehumanization of loss, and rage rise to the surface. Rage connects to the concept of what it means to be a man. After doing all this work, we discuss the insights gained. What can we do to avoid triggers in the future? We talk of our new understanding of what we went through and how we came to be the type of person who could commit these crimes. We examine if we have changed, and if so, what has changed in our lives to give us new perspectives.

I completed both courses before being asked to become a facilitator for the class. Those individuals who can co-facilitate this course with the outside facilitator-volunteer are those who had attended both the basic and advanced courses and whose level of participation was outstanding. These men have become familiar with the goals of emotional awareness and have worked through their own issues. They have been willing to share, both in class and in their writing, on a very deep level about the pain in their background that caused them to act in antisocial ways. They have found meaning in their lives and are able to provide others with a positive role model.

Responsibilities of the facilitator include leading the class discussion of the text, the weekly meditation, and providing moral instruction that may or may not be covered in the text. Facilitators also encourage personal sharing - sharing oneself and being available to class members during the week to offer support and direction. The facilitator must have learned how to regulate their own emotions, especially anger and shame. They must be effective communicators, demonstrate empathy, and practice good listening skills. The facilitator also needs to be comfortable leading the class. Facilitators must not only "talk the talk" but also "walk the walk" of a reflective and genuine lifestyle.

Since writing the aforementioned article on emotional awareness we have come out of Covid protocols. We now have a new outside facilitator, a new Facilitators Guide to work from (we never had the guides in the past). The curriculum is being changed and we have recently created an emotional awareness board. The board consists of several departments and each department is responsible for different tasks and subgroups. We are in the process of creating a Spanish Emotional

Awareness Group to better serve the needs of that community. The Spanish group will be facilitated by native Spanish speakers.

Again, life was pushing me in the direction of teaching and facilitating. I had developed the skills and confidence to convey lessons clearly and concisely so that people were able to feel comfortable. Now that I had learned to live in a spiritual manner, life was putting challenges and opportunities in my path that I was ready and equipped to deal with.

Jericho Circle Project

Jericho Circle's mission is to facilitate healing circles in a correctional setting. These circles support each man in discovering deeper truths, strengthening internal resources, and being authentic and productive. Through group experience, each man develops emotional awareness and increases proficiency in clear communication, trust, and personal integrity. Each man is empowered to define his personal mission, transform his life, and serve his community. Each Jericho Circle group is an eight-week cycle.

As a member of Jericho Circle, I completed three eight-week cycles before enrolling in a Jericho Circle extensive weekend (a weekend retreat with all attendees having completed the eight-week cycles and expected to show up on a deeper level in a safe environment). After doing the extensive weekend, I became a Circle guide. This meant that I served as a group facilitator.

Jericho Circle is based on psychological principles based on Jungian archetypes. This process requires men to get in touch with their deeper feelings as the facilitator helps them to act out the scenarios through role playing. It is hoped that as we re-experience these events, we will gain insight from them.

Jericho Circle requires that outside volunteers come in once a month to help train the guides and facilitators. This was my favorite part because it allowed me the time and safe environment in which to do intimate and personal work. I would eventually leave the group and focus on emotional awareness, but I have nothing but respect for the guys and miss them.

Alternatives to Violence Project

Alternatives to Violence is associated with the religious Society of Friends (Quakers), but it is not a religious program. It has two parts: a basic introductory level and an advanced level. This program is different from the other programs because of the number of participants involved and the number of volunteers and facilitators required. I have done both the basic and advanced levels and have helped to facilitate these programs many times.

The Alternatives to Violence project is formatted as a two-day retreat. The focus of this project is on what they call "transforming power.

Guide to Transforming Power

1. Seek to resolve conflict by reaching common ground.
2. Reach for that something in others that seeks to do good for self and others.
3. Listen. Everyone has made a journey. Try to understand where the other person is coming from before you make up your mind.
4. Base your position on truth. Since people tend to seek truth, no position based on falsehood can long prevail.
5. Be ready to revise your position if you discover it is not fair.
6. When you are clear about your position, expect to experience great inward power to action it. A response that relies on this power will be courageous and without hostility.
7. Do not expect that this response will automatically ward off danger. If you cannot avoid risk, risk being creative rather than violent.
8. Surprise and humor may help transform.
9. Learn to trust your inner sense of when to act and when to withdraw.
10. Work toward new ways of overcoming injustice. Be willing to suffer suspicion, hostility, rejection, and even persecution if necessary.
11. Be patient and persistent in the continuing search for justice.
12. Help build community based on honesty, respect, and caring.

We look at how these principles can help us to avoid violence in the future and how these transforming powers could have helped us resolve issues in the past.

When the agenda is set for the weekend, there will usually be a gathering that will set the tone for the next two days. This consists of speeches or a round robin discussion on a topic. There will be deeply introspective periods of discussion and then possibly "Light and Lively" (silly kid games meant to relax the mood).

Alternating between serious and silly helps to keep people from getting bored. There will be exercises like concentric circles where the participants may do in-depth sharing with other participants they don't know. There are periods where the focus may be on team building and group dynamics, and it is expected that we can come together to reach a common goal. In every group we try to work with affirmation, communication, community building, and conflict resolution. Sometimes we form groups, other times we go deeper with individual work.

Toward the end there is role playing where people act out short skits using conflict resolution. Finally, a debriefing period is followed by graduation.

The first time I got involved in one of these groups, two things stood out. It is hard to see others as threatening and menacing when they are playing childish games with you and laughing their butts off. Second, I was amazed how deep the guys would go in concentric circles with someone they didn't know.

Alcoholics Anonymous / Narcotics Anonymous

AA (Alcoholics Anonymous) and NA (Narcotics Anonymous) are programs that people are familiar with in society. Most people know someone who has benefitted from these programs over the years. Both are based on abstinence, and both have a spiritual component.

I am using them here together, although I tend to focus on alcohol as that played such a big part in my life. The only requirement for membership is a desire to stop drinking alcohol or using drugs.

I had tried AA many times as a young man about nineteen or twenty years old, but I refused to accept anything as my "rock-bottom." I could find a new bottom every time. What do we mean when we talk about hitting the bottom? Well, this can vary for every individual, but it often means we get tired enough of our own suffering so that we decide to make the necessary changes in our lives to stay sober or "clean." No matter how much I was suffering in my teens,

I couldn't envision not drinking. When I tried to stop drinking, my hands got shaky, and my body felt like it was shriveling into a tightly packed bundle of wretchedness. In California, I managed to get sober for a year while participating in AA. I had a sober cousin that participated in AA, and he helped to keep me on the straight and narrow.

That was the most successful and prosperous I had ever been. At nineteen years of age, I had a job making light deliveries in my truck, I had a small apartment, and eventually I moved out to the San Fernando Valley. Maybe because things were going my way, I got cocky and overconfident.

I became involved with a married but separated woman. Her husband was still around with some dirty money behind him. There is a reason AA participants and sponsors tell you not to get involved with someone in the AA program during your first year. It is because most of us are coming from very dysfunctional places and do not have enough life experience to make rational, adult decisions in our lives. I didn't just go out and relapse because I was fooling around with a married woman, but I was setting up the conditions to relapse by pulling away from AA people and getting emotionally involved with someone who was newly sober and wrestling her own demons.

THE TWELVE STEPS OF ALCOHOLICS ANONYMOUS

1) We admitted we were powerless over alcohol—that our lives had become unmanageable.
2) We came to believe that a power greater than ourselves could restore us to sanity.
3) We made a decision to turn our will and our lives over to the care of God as we understand him.
4) We made a searching and fearless moral inventory of our lives.
5) We admitted to God, to ourselves, and to another human being the exact nature of our wrongs.
6) We were entirely ready to have God remove all our defects of character.
7) We humbly asked him to remove our shortcomings.
8) We made a list of all people we had harried and became willing to make amends to them.
9) We made direct amends to such people wherever possible except when to do so would injure them or others.
10) We continued to take personal inventory, and when we were wrong, promptly admitted it.
11) We sought through prayer and meditation to improve our conscious contact with God as we understood Him, praying only for His knowledge for us and the power to carry that out.
12) Having had a spiritual awakening as a result of these steps, we tried to carry this message to alcoholics and to practice these principles in all our affairs.

To someone trying to detox from a bender on the street, these things may sound like very strange concepts. Here is how I applied them:

1) I no longer had a problem admitting that I was powerless over alcohol and that my life had become unmanageable.
2) I did come to believe in a Power greater than myself that could restore me to sanity — unfortunately, it would take me years to find it.
3) Once I had a concept of God that I could work with, I did in fact turn my life over to Him / it.
4) I have had to do searching and thorough moral inventories of myself, and I continue to do so daily.
5) I have done so in many formats, including this book.
6) I believe God has allowed me to work on myself enough to get rid of most of my defects of character with his help.
7) I humbly asked Him to remove my shortcomings.
8) I made a list of those I had harmed and became willing to make amends to all of them.
9) I have made direct amends whenever possible. The second part of that phrase is equally true, and that means not barging into other people's lives when that could cause them great anguish.
10) I am often wrong in my daily life and freely admit it.
11) This is well in keeping with my yoga mindfulness and Buddhist mindset.
12) I try to be a positive influence in all aspects of my life and often try to steer people away from drugs and toward programs.

Why are these programs and others important, you ask? They are extremely important because if a man is going to get out of prison, and he has not seriously reflected on the decisions that brought him there, then he is bound to repeat those actions. Many people are angry at the world, are hostile to education, and refuse to do anything but blame others. All I can say about that is hopefully in the future they look at the reasons they ended up in prison in a more open frame of mind.

These programs are offered because the parole board wants to know that people have reflected on their lives, seen the mistakes they have made, and have considered ways of avoiding those pitfalls in the future. But more than anything they want you to be able to explain to them how you became capable of murder or other crimes. What were the causal factors? How have you addressed them? If you have a violent history, have you addressed the causes of violence? If drugs and alcohol are issues, then have you addressed them? If you have a history of domestic abuse, then how have you dealt with that? In short, parole releases people based on their likelihood to reoffend, and if you have not addressed your issues, then you are staying in prison.

One thing that must be stressed repeatedly is the age at which many come to prison. Most are from extremely poor backgrounds, have little to no education, and have multiple traumas whether that is sexual abuse, physical abuse, emotional abuse, and/or drug and alcohol abuse. They grew up watching friends and family members get murdered in their communities. By the time most people see parole, they have at least 15 to 20 years of incarceration but may have 30-40 years, and are no longer the misguided, reactionary teens they were when they came in. Most have grown up, matured, and hopefully gained insight into their crimes. In the end, these men and women will be getting out and returning to your communities. Do you want well adjusted, mature people who own their actions? Or do you want them as ignorant and hostile as they were when they came in? There is a choice, but it requires supporting prison reform, education, and re-entry programs.

More important than prison reform is sentencing reform. Why?

Because so many of our concepts about murder and justice have been changing in recent years, especially considering the brain science and juvenile justice issues. We now have a ten-year sample as to how the juveniles who were released have fared in society. To this point the studies have proven what the brain science says: juveniles continue to grow and mature in prison, and they grow out of their rashness, hostility, and impulsivity.

Chapter 10

From Darkness to Light

Few people who have read this far will ever question that I was walking on a path of darkness spiritually and mentally. I can't say that I intentionally set out on a path of darkness but that was where I found myself. I guess that is where you end up when you feel completely lost, isolated, alone and when you feel that you are unloved, and the world hates you. None of us set out to become drunks, druggies, thieves, cheats, liars and loners, but far too often that is where people end when they don't seem to make those social connections early in life. I know I never set out to become a bitter, narrow minded, hateful, self-loathing person but that was where I ended up.

I can now understand how I came to be the person I became, I can now see my early childhood trauma through the eyes of an adult. I can see how the lack of love, lack of bonding, lack of social interactions all contributed to the messages I was receiving about myself. I can understand why I felt so utterly worthless and felt that everything was my fault. I can see this now because I have done the work necessary to figuring out the contributing causes that made me the person I became. This does not excuse my actions or my crimes because I am still responsible for my own actions, but it does help explain how they came about. As an adult I had to learn to be forgiving and empathetic to my own inner child because I was just trying to protect myself in a world that seemed so far beyond my understanding.

I need the reader to know that although I had become very callous to the world and the people in it, a lot of that was just a child's way of trying to protect himself. I never became completely amoral, or antisocial I just never expected to fit in naturally with other people. Hidden well inside I did have a moral compass, but it was very repressed. As I began to read more about Buddhism, yoga and, mindfulness I would begin to get more in touch with these aspects of myself.

Most people will never need to walk the same dark path that I did, but everyone has their own crosses to bear, and those burdens can become overwhelming at times. I do not pretend to have a solution to everyone's problems, I can only tell the reader about my path and how and why I made the choices that I did. I did change the direction of my life psychologically, mentally, and spiritually.

In a sense every redemption is the same: overcoming guilt, sins, errors, crimes, shame or other negative qualities, usually with the help of education, spirituality and/or insight.

GOD COME TO EACH OF US, IN HIS OWN WAY, IN HIS OWN TIME

The above was my own quote because I understand that what worked for me may resonate differently for someone else. Many people come to the table with their own ideas as to who and what God is. My purpose is not to engage in a theological debate but to simply inform the reader that God came to me is his own way, in his own time. The reader can do with that what they wish. My spirituality and understanding of God come from a Buddhist, yogic, mindfulness perspective. Many readers in the west may not have a good understanding of these concepts, so I will briefly summarize them before proceeding.

BUDDHISM

Buddhism has no creator deity and gives a leading role to the doctrine of karma. The four noble truths of Buddhism state that (1) all existence is suffering, (2) the cause of suffering is desire, (3) the freedom from suffering is nirvana, and (4) this is attained through the eightfold path of ethical conduct, wisdom, mental discipline and meditation.

THE EIGHTFOLD PATH

The path to Nirvana comprises eight aspects in which an aspirant must become practiced. Right views, intention, speech, action, livelihood, effort, mindfulness and concentration.

YOGA

1) YAMAS: ahimsa, satya, asetya, brahmachara, aparigraha. These are all about personal conduct and ethical rules and are meant to guide us toward harmonious living.

2) NIYAMAS: second limb of eightfold path: saucha, santosha, tapas, svadhyaya, ishvara, and prandihana. This aspect deals with cleanliness, contentment, good discipline, study of self through meditation and surrendering to the divine.

3) ASANA: body postures. The body is a temple; we take care of our body in mind, body and spirit. These are the poses of yoga which everyone is familiar with.

4) PRANAYAMA: ancient breathing techniques. Using our breath to energize and destress as well as to gain mastery over our emotions and bodies

5) PRATYAHAR: fifth limb of yoga. The ability to disengage your mind by controlling your reactions to external disturbances.

6) DHARANA. This deals with the many distractions of the mind and focusing on one thing at a time.

7) DYHANA. Meditation is the uninterrupted flow of soft but steady concentration.

8) SAMADHI. This is the state of bliss. The yogi merges with his or her point of focus and transcends the self. There is a strong connection to the divine

MINDFULNESS

Meditation and mindfulness practices are powerful tools you can use to create peace and calm in your life. Meditation helps you see things more clearly, reduces stress and allows you to live more fully awake and in the present. Practicing mindfulness will help with controlling habitual impulses and reactions that can lead to further problems. It is about training the mind to be awake, stable, peaceful, reflective, and grounded in the moment.

This has been a brief overview of each practice just for the readers edification.

WE ARE BOTH BURDENED AND BLESSED BY THE GREAT RESPONSIBILITY OF FREEWILL AND THE POWER OF CHOICE.

OUR FUTURE IS DETERMINED IN LARGE PART BY THE CHOICES WE MAKE NOW.

WE CANNOT ALWAYS CONTROL OUR CIRCUMSTANCES BUT WE CAN AND DO CHOOSE OUR RESPONSE TO WHATEVER ARISES.

RECLAIMING THE POWER OF CHOICE, WE FIND THE COURAGE TO LIVE FULLY IN THE WORLD.

(from the laws of spirit by Dan Millman)

These concepts were something completely different than what I was used to and when I began to incorporate them in my life things began to change in a very real way. When I lived in society, I believed that God was against me and that people were evil and cruel. How ironic then that I would need to come to prison to find God, kindness, understanding, and a way to live in the world. Even if that world was only one square mile and surrounded by barbed and razor wire fencing.

Even during the height of my insanity, I knew I was not living in accord with my own moral compass. My moral compass had been lost for many years, but when I eventually found it again it still worked. It just needed to be dusted off and have a new directional needle installed.

I spoke already about trying to get my college degree, trying to grow up in prison and trying to navigate my new world when I didn't feel equipped to do so. These concepts of Buddhism, yoga, and mindfulness would become a huge tool for allowing me to do so. They were also speaking to me about trying to live by a code of ethical conduct.

HOW DO THESE CONCEPTS GET APPLIED?

How do these concepts get applied when people are getting stabbed up and thrown off of the tier in the block? That is a very simple but very complicated question. It is complicated because it needs some context. At the time, Walpole was the max and it was a very dangerous place to be. The things that became normalized in that environment were incredible. At the time there were only a couple rules 1) mind your own business 2) shut your mouth 3) don't look in people's cells and 4) the guards are not your friends.

In a sense, it was very easy to accept some of these concepts. For instance, before I became adept at doing meditation, I would simply adopt one mantra or thought for the day. I may just repeat a phrase in my mind all day - like in the eye of the storm find your calm - and when some craziness occurred, I would repeat it to myself, and this would trigger a mindful thought or momentary meditation. I found that I could in fact find my calmness in the storm.

I learned that I could do things to delay the time of reaction to response. One of the most ingenious came from one of my fellow prisoners instead of my yoga masters. He told me when you are face to face with a guard and he is trying to get you to react, simply pause and think about your feet. I thought he was nuts, but a month or so later a guard got in my face trying to provoke me and I paused and thought of my feet. When I realized that I was contemplating my feet rather than reacting to the provocation I started to laugh to myself. The cop asked me what the hell was so God damned funny? He was still in charge, but the power dynamic had shifted just a little bit because I could now at least have some control over the result. I was able to defuse the situation by simply telling him yeah, OK you got that. It was brilliant and simple, and I put forth a lot more effort into reading what the masters of Buddhism, yoga, and mindfulness had to say.

THEY ALL AGREED

Although Buddhism, yoga, and mindfulness strayed from each other in certain respects, the one thing they all agreed on was the concept of meditation. Controlled breathing would be part of the meditation. The first few times I tried to meditate my mind kept racing and I thought I would over amp. I had been reading enough about meditation that I knew this active mind (ego wanting control) was very common and was familiar to all three disciplines. It didn't help much that I had no one to teach me. In any case I can be very determined, and I stayed with it and eventually figured it out. I began to do a little 5-10-minute meditation in the morning before everyone woke up.

I allowed my thoughts to come, recognized them as random thoughts and let them float away. I would then pull my attention back to the present, time and time again. Over time I began to be still, to be present, and to acknowledge what my body was telling me. My thoughts would come and go, and I would draw my attention back to center. Eventually my thought may be about ethical or moral questions and how I was showing up in the world, come back to center, acknowledge my moods, pull it back to center, be quiet, be still, be present. It was a new and interesting concept to me and really helped me become more peaceful.

WHAT ABOUT BUDDHISM?

I thought Buddhism was pretty cool because it didn't really matter what my concept of God was to embrace the things they were talking about. I began to look at the doctrine of karma. There are many schools of Buddha, and some give more focus to certain things than other, but they all shared the notion of karma. I was uncertain about the concept of reincarnation and the repeating cycles of life until you work it all out, but I could embrace the idea of karma. I had been putting straight toxicity into the world for my whole life so it should not have been a surprise that it came back to bite me in the ass. If prison was my present existence for my past actions, then it was my goal in life to work that out. I could believe that all existence is suffering (I always thought so anyways). That the cause of suffering is desire (my desire to be free was causing me to suffer). That freedom from suffering is nirvana (if I could live in the present and stop sweating freedom, I could be content). This is attained by following the eightfold path. Right views, intention, speech, action, livelihood, effort, mindfulness, and concentration. What this meant to me in a very real sense was that I could change my karma by changing my actions. In other words, by acting ethically I could put out positive energy that would not only affect me and those around me but also potentially affect everyone I came in contact with and maybe even the world as a whole.

I began to embrace the concept of psychic energy and psychic healing. I won't get too far into it here but essentially it means that I can have a positive influence on others. That was a pretty big step for a convicted murderer to take!

YOGA

Before I adopted yoga in the form of the asanas (poses) I had already been practicing yoga as a mental and ethical practice. Yoga had rules of ethics and personal conduct. I was embracing concepts like cleanliness, moderation, contentment, and good discipline. I was on board with the breathing exercises and meditation. I was gaining a concept of the divine in a way that made sense to me. Regardless of whatever else was going on around me, if I was conducting myself in an ethical manner, I could be content in that moment, and the future and past didn't seem to matter as much. I would eventually incorporate the asanas and it just felt like the natural extension of what I was already doing. Today we are attempting to bring a yoga teacher certification program into the prison although it hasn't happened yet.

MINDFULNESS

I like the idea of mindfulness and I was already doing the meditation anyway so adding focus to it was relatively easy. I would wake up every morning when the rest of the block still slept, and I would do a meditation to start the day. It didn't need to be long - 10-15 minutes would usually suffice. At the end of the meditation, I would set an intention for the day. Most days it would be something pro-social like "let me be less judgmental today."

HOW DID IT HELP

One thing I learned about meditation was that it allowed me to alter my neural pathways. For instance, by repeating the same negative thoughts, reactions, and emotions over and over, it entrenches these things in your brain. However, when we meditate and our minds begin to wander, when we pull our focus back to the present, we weaken those negative neural pathways. If I feel that I am being triggered for anger, I can pull my focus back to centering myself, I can then choose to feel joy or compassion instead. By doing so, I strengthen the positive pathways and weaken the negative ones and eventually over time it gets easier and easier to do. I would also want to choose positive emotions because carrying around so much anger and hate is physically exhausting.

After spending my first 10-15 years in prison I was no longer a kid. I no longer acted rashly and impulsively. I began to learn how to speak to people and how to act like an adult. I was no longer having problems with guards or other prisoners, and I noticed that most days I was beginning to feel good about myself. I liked being consistent in my moods, I liked not having problems with others and I liked the way I was beginning to show up in the world.

WERE THERE ANY OTHER BENEFITS?

Yes. After thirty plus years George and I ended up in the same prison. We had gone our own ways and done our separate things but when we were thrust back together, we would need to forgive each other and have compassion and empathy for each other. He was now a gray-haired grandfather and I was growing gray, teaching and just heading into the beginnings of old age. We could not have the type of friendship we had in our twenties but nor were we looking to cause each other harm. We had grown in our own ways, and that is why it is in this chapter dealing with spirituality.

I could also no longer write off spirituality as just something I study. It had become a way of life and that meant I had come to see gods hand in it. The divinity, the spirit, the oneness, the always present, however you want to define it. Where I used to hate myself, I came to love myself. Where I was narrow-minded, I became open minded. Where I had been scornful and judgmental of others, I had become accepting and non-judgmental. I was now able to have compassion and empathy for others. Eventually I had it for myself as well and for the little boy inside of me who couldn't protect himself as a child.

When I first got into this spirituality stuff I could not have predicted where it would lead. I had always walked in darkness and stumbled many times on the path. I guess I just needed to be kicked in the head enough times and dragged off to the hole enough times to finally get the message. I have changed every aspect of my former self and I have these ethical paths to thank for it.

COMPASSION FOR YOUR OPPRESSOR

It took me a long time to understand this concept. Each discipline spoke of it, but I wasn't understanding it. Many times, I would have liked some payback for the guards beating me up. I had also come to the point of understanding that I needed to forgive them for beating me up. I really was an obnoxious asshole who brought a lot of misery on myself. I also knew I didn't want that kind of anger consuming me and weighing me down, so I had actually let it go. It felt good to be rid of it!

I knew there was a lesson here that I needed to learn so I did what I always do, I went in search of answers in books. I read books on Nelson Mandela, the Dalai Lama, Martin Luther King, Mahatma Ghandi. Each of these people had said something along similar lines and all of them would have been justified in their hate and anger yet each of them said the same thing: you must have compassion for your oppressor.

One day, Billy and I were walking the track when 3-4 guards were having a discussion in front of a housing unit. They were complaining about guard union politics, about how all of the inmate scum should be eradicated, and how nobody appreciates them.

Billy and I began our own discussion because he had been around for decades as well. Billy how is it that these guys go home at night, are some of the highest paid guards in the nation, they do nothing for work, can't be fired yet they are more miserable than you and me and we have decades in prison? Then I suddenly got what the masters had been talking about. I had forgiven them and let my anger go and I felt free, but they were consumed by hate, locked in their positions and saw no wrong in it. I now understood when Martin Luther King said LET NO MAN BRING YOU LOW ENOUGH TO HATE HIM.

This doesn't only apply to the guards, because some of our guys could never see the humanity in a guard even if he just did his job and went home. I think they could ALL use some yoga and forgiveness, but each man must find his own path.

All of the obstacles on my path from darkness to light were just God's way of trying to get my attention. I have had more obstacles than I would wish on anybody, but I have also been granted the strength to overcome those obstacles. Now I choose to be a beacon for others to follow so they can see the path of light for themselves.

THE WARRIOR OF LIGHT CONCENTRATES ON THE SMALL MIRACLES OF DAILY LIFE. HE IS CAPABLE OF SEEING WHAT IS BEAUTIFUL BECAUSE HE CARRIES BEAUTY WITHIN HIMSELF, FOR THE WORLD IS A MIRROR AND GIVES BACK TO EACH MAN A REFLECTION OF HIS OWN FACE.

THE WARRIOR KNOWS HIS OWN FAULTS AND LIMITATIONS, BUT HE DOES ALL HE CAN TO MAINTAIN HIS GOOD HUMOR IN MOMENTS OF CRISIS. THE WORLD IS, AFTER ALL, DOING IT'S BEST TO HELP HIM, EVEN THOUGH EVERYTHING AROUND HIM SEEMS TO BE SAYING THE OPPOSITE.

(PAOLO COELHO, The Warrior of light.)

Remember what your mom said about being careful what you post online? That was essentially what happened on the day I got convicted I was labeled forever by that action. I have tried to atone for that in the only way I know how. I have made every attempt to become a different person than I was on the street, that is the only way I know of that I can at least honor my victim.

Chapter 11

Backing Out of the Deal

What are we talking about when we say that there was a deal to reduce the verdict in my sentence from 1st degree murder (life without parole) to a 2nd degree life sentence with parole eligibility after 15 years?

Under Massachusetts rules of criminal conduct 25 (b) (2) the judge can use his or her own discretion to reduce a verdict if he believes the verdict may not be consistent with justice. The other way this works is when the district attorney's office and the defense counsel can make a stipulated agreement that the verdict was not consistent with justice.

As spoken of in earlier chapters I had signed an affidavit in 1986 and again in 1993 to the effect that my counsel at trial was ineffective for not explaining to me the difference between first-degree murder and second-degree murder prior to trial, especially in regard to extreme atrocity and cruelty. It was not until we were two weeks into the trial that my attorney approached me in the holding cell and explained the difference between the two charges. He said that although there were no weapons or intent to kill that the jury could find me guilty by reason of extreme atrocity or cruelty. He then went on to explain that the difference between the two was that with a first-degree life sentence I would never be eligible for parole but with a second-degree life sentence I would become parole eligible after 15 years. He asked if I would be willing to plead guilty to a second-degree life sentence.

I told my lawyer at that moment "go make that happen" (pleading guilty to second-degree murder). He left for a about 5 minutes and then returned telling me that, "The D.A.'s office won't go for it now because we are two weeks into the trial, and they couldn't do that to the victim's family at that point."

My question in all of this has always been "Shouldn't he have explained this to me before trial so that I could plead guilty to a reduced charge rather than explaining it to me midway through the trial?"

So how did my lawyer's actions from 1984 come to be an issue in 2016 when I was trying to resolve this issue in the courts? It came to be an issue years later because a case had been decided years after my conviction which changed the law. This law affected me and applied to what I had been saying about my lawyer's ineffectiveness.

The Marinho decision is cited in Commonwealth V. Marinho 464 Mass 115 (2013) and is longer and more in depth than the average reader needs to know or concern themselves with but to summarize why this applied to me I offer the following.

In addition to the record of the new trial motion that I had filed and was pending with the court, I submitted my own affidavit, an affidavit from the trial prosecutor (which is virtually unheard of), and a memorandum of law in support of my reduction motion. I included with that an affidavit from attorney Greg Shubert, as it contained evidence that spoke to the Marinho factors. The affidavits and memoranda set forth the reason why the parties had reached an agreement to reduce the verdict. There was a reasonable probability that the district attorney's office would have offered a deal, that I would have accepted that deal, and that the trial judge would have permitted a guilty plea to second-degree murder prior to trial if defense counsel had provided effective assistance of counsel at the pre-trial plea-bargaining stage of the case.

Why would I be entitled to relief? To establish prejudice as to counsel's deficient performance I needed to show a reasonable probability that the result would have been more favorable than the outcome at trial. There is no question on these facts showing that the result would have been more favorable as I was convicted of first-degree murder with no possibility of parole. The result of a plea to second-degree would have made me eligible for parole after fifteen years. I have now been incarcerated for 38 years and done in essence two second-degree life sentences.

What about overcoming prejudice? To establish prejudice, it is not only necessary for a defendant to prove a reasonable probability that a plea would have resulted in a more favorable outcome. The defendant must demonstrate a reasonable probability that the prosecution would have made an offer, the offer would have been accepted, and the court would have approved the deal. While proof of prejudice cannot be based on mere speculation or conjecture as to outcome. A reasonable probability is one sufficient to undermine the confidence of the outcome, it does not mean more likely than not.

What were the components that I needed to satisfy to reach my claim?

1) That the prosecution would have offered the plea to second-degree if my attorney asked for it.
2) That I would have accepted it.
3) That the court would have allowed it.

The record supports each component as follows:

A) My trial attorney never mentioned or instructed me on a plea to second-degree murder until two weeks into the trial.
B) If my trial attorney had sought a plea to second-degree, the trial prosecutor would have accepted it.
C) The trial prosecutor asserted that a pre-trial second-degree plea would have been aligned with the practice and policy of the District Attorney's office at that time.
D) The trial prosecutor would have made this deal despite the objections of the victim's family, and he believed that it would have been approved.
E) The prosecuting attorney's viewpoint as to how the District Attorney's office saw the case was bolstered by the affidavit of attorney Greg Shubert who had dealings with the D.A.'s office about this case in 1988.
F) The trial prosecutor reviewed and signed an affidavit stating that a plea to second-degree would not have been contingent on approval from the victim's family.

Would I have accepted a second-degree plea?

G) Through my own affidavit I have answered this in the affirmative.
H) When my trial attorney explained the difference between first-degree (no parole) and second-degree (parole possibility after 15 years) halfway through the trial I told him to go make that happen (a plea to second-degree).

I) The trial prosecutor corroborated the fact that for the first time, in the middle of the trial, he was approached about a second-degree murder but at that point it was too late.

Would the court have approved the offer?

J) The prosecuting attorney believed that his boss, District Attorney John Conte would have accepted the offer since he never denied District Attorney Aloise's recommendation. He further believed that Judge Travers would have accepted it as he allowed prosecutors and defense attorneys to resolve their own differences. The judge would have given the victim's family time to be heard but it would not hold him back from agreeing to it.

This was what it took to satisfy Marinho.

This is why the District Attorney's office and defense counsel had agreed to reduce the verdict.

What about the stipulated agreement?

In January 2019 the case was called for a status hearing. The judge noted two agreed upon motions to reduce the verdict had been filed and that the Commonwealth was going to submit stipulated facts, the ADA King stated that the stipulated facts would not be to the underlying offense but would be to an agreement that they were constrained by the affidavit of the former prosecutor, and they felt, "They have no legal recourse in terms of opposing the reduction in sentence."

THAT WAS PRETTY REMARKABLE THAT THE DISTRICT ATTORNEY'S OFFICE CONCEDED THAT THEY COULD NOT WIN THE CASE.

What did we agree to?

We said 1) this reduction is a satisfactory resolution to my Rule 30 Motion. 2) the parties agreed to stipulated facts in lieu of live testimony and that this may constitute the basis for supporting the motion. My affidavit was submitted, an affidavit for the trial prosecutor, and a memorandum of law in support of the motion for reduction in verdict. The defense asserted, and the Commonwealth conceded, that the record of this case contains evidence of a reasonable probability that the D.A.'s office would have offered, that the defendant would have accepted, and that the trial judge would have allowed a guilty plea to second-degree to be entered prior to trial had defense counsel provided effective assistance of counsel at pre-trial stage.

Okay, so what happened?

We went to court several times and each time the District Attorney kept telling the judge that the victim's family doesn't want to be there. The judge kept insisting that they should be there and have the opportunity to speak and be heard. ADA King informed the judge that the family simply wanted this done quietly so as not to draw any attention from the press and to respect the families wishes. The father would not come down from Maine and he would not participate no matter what county it was heard in.

Judge Sullivan stated, "That makes all the sense in the world." The judge said if the parties wanted to do the please on the same day to spare the victim's family, that he had no problem doing that.

At the next hearing on October 24th, 2018, ADA King explained that the Commonwealth has agreed to a Rule 25 (b) reduction in the first-degree murder conviction to a second-degree murder conviction. Judge Sullivan agreed. The judge then mentioned the victim's family again. ADA King stated he had spoken to the victim's father in Maine and that he is unable to travel. ADA King then mentioned a half-sister who wasn't on the victim notification, and she stated that neither she nor her father wanted to participate in this process.

Judge Sullivan stated, "I thought someone was going to be here from the victim's family?" ADA King stated she told him at the last hearing that no one from the family would be coming and stated the reasons why. This was echoed by my attorney. ADA King stated that the family has told her they did not want to be here today and that they don't want to play any part in this. Judge Sullivan again reiterated his belief that someone from the family would be there, although there is nothing in the record supporting that belief. Judge Sullivan once again put it on the District Attorney's office to produce the victim's family in court.

Judge Sullivan had dragged this on for a few years always moving the goalposts on us and setting new conditions while all the time telling us he was going to do it, that he saw no reason not to do it, that he knew what we were looking for (relief) and had even said we were going to do it. He completely changed his position on us.

Once again, the family wanted no part in it. The judge went back into court and started picking apart the weakness of our case as presented to the point that when the D. A.'s office saw that the judge was now opposed to doing this reduction that they pulled their offer for a reduction of sentence.

Judge Sullivan asked ADA King, "Why are you pulling your reduction of sentence motion?" and her reply was "BECAUSE OF EVERYTHING YOU SAID YOUR HONOR." This meant that the sitting judge, instead of being an arbiter of the proceedings had instead become a prosecutor of them. That was why the District Attorney's office withdrew their offer.

I am just a layman when it comes to law, but it seems to me that if the judge is unwilling to trust the D.A.'s office to make a good judgement in the interest of justice that really is an indictment of the Worcester District Attorney's office.

So, what did the original prosecuting attorney have to say?

In summary of the original trial prosecutor's affidavit, it states as follows:

Affidavit from attorney Louis Aloise:

1) That he was the prosecutor of my case.
2) That he would listen to defense attorneys who would approach him about pleas.
3) That he would consult with his boss if he felt a plea was in the best interest of the D.A.'s office.
4) That they would consult with the victim's family, they considered the degree of culpability and the characteristics of both the victim and the family.
5) That my trial counsel approached him about a manslaughter plea and never discussed with him a plea to second-degree.
6) Aloise believed that the worst he could do with my case was a manslaughter conviction, so he saw no reason to plead it to manslaughter.
7) That my lawyer did not approach him about a second-degree until two weeks into a trial at which point it was too late.
8) That if my trial attorney had approached him prior to trial that he would have been willing to do so after consulting with his boss.
9) That this would have been in alignment with office policy and practices at the time.

10) That they would always consider the victim's family sentiments but that the family's wishes would not be the deciding factor in a plea.
11) Although the victim's family would have been upset, he still would have advocated for a second-degree.
12) He believed this case was the type of case that would have resolved with a second-degree plea and that his boss would have allowed it.
13) That Aloise had practiced in front of Judge Travers routinely. He believed that Judge Travers would have allowed it even over the strenuous objections of the victim's family.
14) That he had reviewed my affidavit signed in 1983 and that the contents are accurate, and that the plea would not have been contingent on the victim's family approval.
15) That he is now providing this affidavit in support of my Rule 30 (b) motion of reduction of sentence.
16) Bearing in mind that the Marinho factors speak to what the standards are to warrant relief, it is his belief that the Commonwealth would have offered relief, had my lawyer sought it through pre-trial plea bargaining and that he believes the court would have allowed it.

So, the judge backed out of our stipulated agreement, had forced the D.A.'s office to retract their offer and now I would need to go forward on the Rule 30 in front of a different judge. I knew I was going to be calling a witness who was a friend of Judge Sullivan's so I asked that he be recused from my case as he had already shown his intent to shoot me down.

The only question I had going forward was if he had already tainted the well because I knew that the next judge would be examining his decision.

I was now assigned a Judge Reardon to hear my case going forward. The hearing would take place in stages because we needed to call witnesses during the height of the Covid pandemic. We called Louise Aloise who was the District Attorney who prosecuted me back in 1983. He testified to everything laid out in the affidavit from the previous pages.

We next called Ed Ryan who was a long-time lawyer in Worcester and was around in the days when I went on trial and had inside knowledge of how the District Attorney's office ran at the time and had been friends with Judge Travers. His opinion was that Judge Travers would have allowed the plea to second-degree if my trial attorney and the former D.A. thought that it was an equitable solution and was agreed on by both parties.

My testimony would include my childhood, upbringing, issues with alcoholism and drug addiction. I spoke about joining the Marines in an attempt to straighten out my life, of going to rehab and A.A. in an attempt to get sober. I also spoke about my lack of ability to hold a job as a youth or have any real ties in the community.

We then went into the night of the crime and for the first time in my life I owned my actions publicly. I thought that the judge had been paying attention and listening intently but when he ultimately made his decision it was against me. I sincerely thought we should have won on the Marinho argument or that the judge should have granted relief under Rule 25 (b)(2), a verdict more consistent with justice.

I felt that having already served 35 years at that time, in conjunction with brain science studies, I should have warranted a reduction in sentence especially since my prison record identified a total turn-around of my behavior.

I spoke about gaining my college degree, teaching a man to read and write, growing up in prison under adverse conditions and how I have matured and changed. I spoke about holding a job for decades while in prison. I spoke of learning a second language, finding my voice in Toastmasters, and of becoming a teacher and facilitator to all my program groups.

The judge asked, "what does that entail facilitating a group in prison?" I was able to tell him that we attempt to look at the effects of childhood trauma to help us gain a better understanding as to how we become the type of people capable of taking someone's life. I spoke briefly about the masks we wear (the loner, the Rebel etc.) come to define how we see ourselves and relate to the world but that we try to look behind the masks to determine what the traumas are and to realize that they no longer serve us as adults.

In the judge's decision, he credited the testimony of attorney Aloise and Ryan and credited my testimony in part. By calling into question my creditability it gave the judge an easy out. Judge Reardon simply used udge Traver's opinion from twenty years before although there has never been one thing in the record to question my creditability on.

It was hugely disappointing and now I must pick up the pieces of my life and go forward as best I can.

Chapter 12
Licking My Wounds

After being shot down in court, I felt as though life had thoroughly kicked me in the balls, and it just took all the life out of me. I needed to lock myself in my cell for about two weeks to process what had happened and what it meant. I had spent several years thinking my sentence was going to be reduced only to have my hopes and dreams blow up in my face. I had been planning on how I was going to go forward with the last part of my life in a manner different that how I lived the first part of my life.

I knew what it meant. It meant that I was now probably going to die in prison. It also meant that no matter what my feelings were about being shot down that I would need to stop feeling sorry for myself, pick myself up off the floor, and go forward in the best manner that I could.

This is the nature of serving a life without parole sentence. No matter what happens in life, no matter who dies, or what adversity you have to deal with, there is no time off. There are no vacations, holidays, sick days, weekends at the spa or hikes in the mountains. Because of this, lifers become very adept at dealing with tough issues head on, as there is no avoiding difficult subjects. We become very adept at compartmentalizing things. We find ways to deal with our tensions and frustrations or they can overwhelm us and cause us serious mental health issues. I channel these issues into meditation, yoga, and exercise. I have been taking a SYDA YOGA course through the mail for years and by the time it arrives it usually helps me refocus my attention and live in the present.

In the wake of me being shot down in court I needed to really look at my life and reconcile who I am, with who I was when I came into prison. It is like looking at completely different lives. I needed to keep in mind that I am still in prison almost 40 years later because I killed someone. There was no real reason for him to die that night or his family to lose their son. I can't get away from that fact and wishing it wasn't so doesn't help.

I can look back on my early years now and see all the contributing factors that led to my becoming the type of person who could take someone's life. That is because I have grown up, taken responsibility, and looked seriously and in depth at exactly how I became that person. None of us set out to become murderers. My story is a sad and tragic tale of a kid from the right side of the tracks, born to a two-parent household, in a safe neighborhood seemingly with everything going for me in life. SO, WHAT HAPPENED?

Contrary to the way things looked from the outside the house was very dysfunctional. My folks were active alcoholics who raised their two sets of children with different messaging and different expectations. I have looked long and hard at the question: did my folks correctly identify the two bad kids and the two good kids and treat them accordingly, or did they cause them to become that way by raising them differently? Me and Denise became drunks, druggies, convicts and struggled in school while having no friends. Val and Jon became medical professionals with productive lives, good friends who excelled in school and had strong friendships. I can speculate that my mom felt Jon and Val were a better reflection of her than were me and Denise. I spoke with a lisp, had learning disabilities and struggled with school and never fit in socially. I can now see that always moving, changing schools and being the new kid didn't help as I always had to fight the new local bully.

When the day came that my mom told me she wished I was never born it changed the path of my life and I never recovered. At the time it confirmed what I already felt coming from my mom which was resentment. It is possible she was just momentarily angry and lashed out at me in frustration, but I completely internalized the message that I was not wanted.

It was at this time that I started drinking and drugging. Pouring alcohol onto lack of love and self-hate was a truly volatile combination that I carried into my teens. I believe I was instantly an alcoholic because when I was completely hammered was the only time I felt no pain. I knew that other people didn't drink the same way I did. Junior high and high school were just places I went to either buy or sell drugs depending on what was around. I rejected people before they could reject me and I took on the loner/rebel facade which I felt at least gave me some kind of power (dysfunctional as it may have been).

I would join the marines, do a geographical move, go to AA, go to rehab and detox trying to address my alcohol issues but I couldn't beat it, I wasn't ready. I became a despicable and pathetic character with nothing going for me, who preyed on vulnerable, weak people wherever he could. I never really had the bully mentality because I had been bullied, but If I could screw someone over, cheat them, take advantage of them or steal from them I would do so. By the time I got arrested for this murder I had become a savage. I had no regard for anybody or anything. I completely hated myself and felt about a thousand years old. I may never have anticipated killing someone but in hindsight I can't say that I am completely surprised it happened either. I have had so much time to reflect on my life and I knew that if this book was going to have any merit whatsoever that I would need to deal honestly with who I was, how I thought, and how I came to change.

The second phase of my life was essentially from the time I went to prison until about age forty. The lost child would grow into a broken man in prison. I wasn't a man when I came to prison, I was a child. I got arrested at 21 and convicted at 22 but boy was I ever immature, with a bad attitude and a lot to learn.

In hindsight and with the benefit of the brain science, I now have a lot better idea as to what was going on with me at the time. I was very rash, impulsive, confrontational, and immature. Walpole at the time was a very dangerous place and I had no idea how to operate in that environment. All I can tell the reader is that when violence is ever present that you learn how to adapt really quick, or you perish. The politics of the place, the chaos, the violence and the things that became normalized in that environment were crazy.

I would crash out a few times (have problems) with some of my fellow prisoners but mostly I would have problems with the guards. There were only a few rules you needed to know (1) mind your own business, (2) shut your mouth, (3) don't look in people's cells and (4) the guards are not your friends.

Once I heard that college courses may be coming into the prison I decided to enroll if the opportunity presented itself. I was always in and out of segregation, and this was where I would meet like-minded men who hated being defined by the press as animals and savages. As each man was released back to population, they all enrolled in college, each man graduated, and none of the men that I met in ten block who graduated ever came back to prison.

That is why I so firmly believe in education. Each man wanted to defiantly prove to the system that they were better than the narrative being written about them. That defiance became their power. It was the first time any of us had channeled defiance into something positive, but it was a lesson I learned well.

I didn't know it at the time, but that same defiance to authority would become my primary teaching tool in the years to come. I knew that every man in prison has been labelled and defined by those in power as animals and savages, that every man has been demeaned, debased, belittled, and looked down on with scorn by those in power. It is actually pretty easy to motivate someone to be better by showing them respect and letting know they are seen. To prove those in power wrong and show them that you are not a monster, but a person who has made a poor decision. This is the difference between immaturity in your twenties and being in control of your life in your 40's, 50's and 60's. This is the difference between using your anger constructively and being used by your anger in a destructive manner. This is the difference between an immature brain and a mature brain.

I wish these lessons could have been learned the easy way, but I guess at that point in my life I was simply not ready to learn yet. I would slowly learn how to be less confrontational, less abrasive, more polite and more tactful. If I had more life experience, better problem-solving skills or less of an attitude, I could have avoided all those problems at the time. Those things that were so overwhelming for me then, are so easily avoided today. I have no bad attitude today and most of my dealings are cordial and peaceful.

This was the period where I taught a man to read and write and I believe that teaching him was one of my first real periods of personal growth. It was certainly the first time that I did something for altruistic reasons. This would begin a long and slow transition into eastern philosophy, Taoism, Buddhism, Yoga, and mindfulness. It would take several years to fully bloom but the seeds had been planted and were beginning to take root.

I think that at a certain point in time, I just became aware that my anger was hurting me more than anyone else. I was finding ways to give anger less and less power over me. As I did so, I began to realize that my dealings with others were becoming much more civil and I no longer had negative interactions with others.

Most of my days were spent working and that way I could occupy my time and have very little interaction with the day shift. I enjoyed work and put together many years working in prison industries. I developed a good work ethic and enjoyed making my own money even if it wasn't much. I never would ask my family for money when I could get by on my own. I knew they would help if I asked but I tried not to ask. I wish I could have found some sort of work ethic when I was on the street, but again, maybe I just wasn't ready. It seems I will learn life's lessons but only after beating my head on the wall for a good long time.

Everything that I had begun learning in the max would really begin to flourish when I arrived at Norfolk and surrounded myself with positive people. Yoga, mindfulness, Toastmasters, learning Spanish, becoming a teacher, participating in and then facilitating programs, these were all things that were becoming bigger parts of my life. The last twenty years I have really grown into the type of person I want to be. I am a lot more conscious of quality of life and the energy I am carrying as well as my mental attitude about things. The person I am today is so vastly different from the one who walked through the prison doors decades ago. I still work, do programs, teach, and try to live as best I can. I hope tomorrow will be a better day.

SO, WHAT NOW?

Now I advocate for myself. I believe I have already done that by telling you who I was and who I am. I have owned all my faults and didn't let them define me. I have overcome many adversities and accomplished so much more than I was supposed to be able to. I believe my story of growth, change, and rehabilitation shows exactly the type of change that is possible in prison

when someone truly wants to do so. In some ways I may be unique, but in others, I am just one face of all the other nameless, faceless people who pass through these walls all the time. Each man is full of possibility and can be their own redemption story if or when given the chance.

When the brain science changed the fate of many young men, I really began to ask myself if these men should have been doing life without parole sentences from the beginning? Should they really have been sentenced for having unformed brains that are fundamentally different from adults? I began to question the point of life without parole sentences? I know first-hand that my own experience tracks exactly with what the brain science predicts will happen to juvenile and youthful offenders. I was immature, hostile, rash, impulsive, lacking processing skills, and prone to violence. As I matured, I became less rash, impulsive, hostile, gained better reasoning and communication skills, and eventually became a fairly well adapted, well-adjusted person. I am no longer prone to criminal activity. The reader can clearly discern the change that has occurred in my life.

When the brain science decided the Miller case, the medical people lacked long-term longitudinal studies to speak about people other than juveniles, although they thought it applied to older teens and young adults as well. They now have ten years of studies that reinforces what their earlier studies predicted. I am in the 18-21-year age group that they call late adolescence, and the bran science should apply to me as well. The courts know this issue is coming and needs to be addressed but so far, they have been unwilling to bump up the age.

I believe I am the perfect example of what rehabilitation and growth are supposed to look like. There is a case pending in the S.J.C. awaiting final disposition which deals with the elimination of life without parole for 18-20-year-olds. COMM V. ROBINSON S.J.C.# 09265 and COMM V. MATTIS S.J.C. # 11693

If this case gets finalized, it will do away with life without parole sentences for 18-20-year-olds. So, the question becomes, why wouldn't you extend it to 21? 18-20-year-olds are in the same age range of the 18-21 age group called late adolescents. I am advocating for myself because I haven't seen any lawyers advocating for the 18-21-year-old age group. Most lawyers know the courts are very conservative and probably figure they will try to move the bar a little at a time instead of asking for too much. I don't have a lawyer advocating for me, no one seems to be advocating for 21-year-olds so I will advocate for myself. I am 60 years old, and my clock is winding down so why not put my Toastmaster skills to use and be my own advocate?

The District Attorney had already offered to reduce my sentence, the man who prosecuted me offered to help me and said it would have been the right thing to do then and it is the right thing to do now. He also spoke to my lawyer's ineffectiveness. I have served almost 40 years and own my actions. I regret the decision that cost a man his life and publicly apologize to his family for my callous and cowardly actions. Nothing I can do will bring him back but maybe in his own way he would be pleased to know that I have made every effort in life to no longer be that person.

Is the only reason the state wants to keep me in prison until I die to teach me the lesson that killing is wrong? I knew that 40 years ago. If the state really wants me to die here, they should have just shot me in the head in the bull pen once I was convicted. It would have saved the state lots of money, put an end to my misery, my family would have moved on long ago and there would be no recidivism whatsoever, and it would have satisfied that unquenchable lust for vengeance.

WHAT DOES IT COST TO INCARCERATE SOMEONE?

I don't have any recent stats, but I remember seeing about 15 years ago that it costs $45,000 dollars a year to incarcerate someone. I believe that number is a very conservative estimate, but I will use it for instructional purposes. At the rate of $45,000 a year for 35 years it has already cost the state $ 1,750,000 to incarcerate me. If it keeps me another 20 years until I die it will have cost the state $2,700,000 not including medical and geriatric costs. For that money we could educate a whole class of kids, could feed the homeless, pay for diversionary programs or run drug and alcohol programs. It could fund a jobs program or help pay for peoples heat in the winter. Is vengeance really worth that? Do we as a nation want to be in favor of vengeance, retribution and death or should we be in favor of life, hope, possibility, and redemption? Should a state ever favor death over life, to prove that killing is wrong? What kind of twisted logic is that?

By the time this book comes to publication, the cases of COMM V. Robinson and COMM V. Mattis will probably have been decided and life without parole will no longer exist for 18-20-year-olds. It is possible the court could extend the age range in accordance with the brain science on their own. What they may do however is rule on the 18-20-yearold category now, while suggesting to the legislature that they draft some kind of legislation up to and including 25-year-old people. The legislature may be inclined to support this because it would be driven by the brain science.

It must be remembered that none of these sentencing changes have occurred because the public is suddenly sympathetic towards these young offenders. It is being done because juvenile and youthful offender's brains are fundamentally different than adults. I personally think the state should do away with life without parole sentences anyways. I have seen hundreds of cases reversed, I have seen hundreds reversed due to D.N.A. evidence, and in recent years Massachusetts has exonerated dozens of people. Most of these were cases from 20, 30, 40, and 50 years ago. These were not overturned on a technicality, they were overturned because police and prosecutors were withholding information, lying, and knowingly continuing to hold people in prison on false or circumstantial evidence.

What is the point of incarcerating someone until they are blind, crippled, crazy, and dealing with Alzheimer's disease or shitting their diapers? I would suggest that the first 10-15 years of a life sentence actually has a punishment value, because you are still adjusting to losing your freedom and getting accustomed to prison. In that time, you either begin to grow up and take responsibility for your actions or you do not. Once someone gets fully acclimated to prison and settles into the routine it loses its punishment value.

My question is, what is the value of punishment when punishment has lost its value? What the public doesn't seem to realize is that these kids are not simply walking out the door, they are serving at least 15 years before becoming parole eligible. Many have served 30 years or more and some may never go home because parole eligibility does not ensure release, it only assures a hearing. This would be the case regardless of if they changed it to 21 or 25-year-olds.

What would happen if the legislature did away with life without parole for people up to 21 years old (late adolescents) or people 22-25 (young adults)? They would have two options. The courts could resentence all of them to life without parole sentences or give them all Miller type mitigation hearings. The state could either do away with life without parole sentences completely (and it is probably time to address that) or leave it intact for those 25 and over.

This would allow the state to address the brain science under the evolving standards of justice premise. I have used my own life as an example of what change and rehabilitation can look like in prison. I hope the events and circumstances of my life make me the face of innovative strategies for updated judicial assessments for 21-year-olds due to the brain science. I hope that I have done enough to prove that I have been and can be rehabilitated. I have acknowledged my faults, owned my addictions, and admitted my crime. I have grown up in prison under some very harsh conditions and become a fairly well adapted teacher, mentor, facilitator, and tutor. I have found the courage to not only advocate for myself but to advocate for others in similar circumstances and who lack the courage and the voice to advocate for themselves. I am simply a man, a representative sample of countless thousands of others who lack a voice, not because they have nothing to say but because they lack someone willing to listen.

Are there other ways that this could be addressed? Yes, they could do mandatory parole. This would entail every man getting out after the minimum 15 years and the state keeps a leash on them by adding conditions of parole in case they violate and need to be brought back.

Presumptive parole is a little different because it means you are presumed to receive parole unless you commit new crimes in prison (these are usually stabbings, assaults and introduction of drugs). This is a powerful management tool for the D.O.C. because if people want to get out of prison they need to comply.

Another idea that has been suggested is something called a 25-50. This means if you have served 25 years (the punishment factor) and are 50 years old you are entitled to release. This recognizes that most people age out of crime and rash, impulsive behaviors. One other thing I heard mentioned is a second chance act. From what I heard of this, it states as long as you are in the brain science age group (25) and have not been granted a life without parole sentence you should be granted a hearing to show you deserve a second chance.

Many of the restorative justice, social justice, criminal justice, sentencing reform people, and attorneys could back this because it still punishes those responsible. What it also does though, is it supports racial justice because many of those convicted of extreme atrocity and cruelty are disproportionately black and brown skinned people. The same is true of joint venture murders. Our governmental institutions of police, courts, and prisons are inherently biased and have been shown historically to abuse the levers of power and social control. Make no mistake about it prisons are a means of social control.

Most prison advocates, restorative justice, and social justice advocates (and even growing numbers of criminal justice people) know that there are many social factors in their communities that contribute to people becoming criminals such as poverty, violence, lack of education, broken families, racism, lack of hope etc. On the individual level there is sexual, physical, emotional abuse. Other factors such as lack of love or support, bullying, drugs, alcohol abuse, social isolation, gangs etc.

When prisoners and restorative justice people work together it is pretty incredible. We come to understand their pain, the harm we have caused, and all the factors that contributed to us becoming the kind of people who could take a life. They come to know our pain, traumas, circumstances, addictions, and family issues that lead us to become such broken people. They know that we are doing prison programs trying to not only figure out what happened in our lives but also how we can change and break the cycle of violence in our communities.

It is a very powerful and emotional thing to sit across from a man or woman who has lost a son to murder and see the type of pain we have caused. This is particularly true when you have caused someone's murder and the guilt and shame suddenly sit with you differently. Currently there is no victim/offender dialogue permitted through either the District Attorney's office or through a D.O.C. mediator. I think this could be very healing and cathartic. Maybe a victim's family would just want answers or to vent their anger. Maybe they would get to forgiveness at some point. Maybe it would be good to let the perpetrator feel the guilt and shame of what he has done. Maybe he would apologize or turn his life around? In either case I think it is a noble idea to consider. I also think that this could be done through victims advocate office if both parties were willing.

I would like to close this book speaking to those who are still in the world suffering, lost and alone thinking no one understands them. I have been there and feel your pain. It is a tough stage of life to get through, but I would rather try to reach you before you come to prison rather than changing your mind set once you are here. I have given the reader a highly sanitized version of what it means to be in prison and need you to know it is worse than described. There are some things that the government at local, state, and national levels do not do well, and the first of those is looking out for the interests of the poor, downtrodden, and disenfranchised. Imagine putting George Floyd, Breonna Taylor, Trayvon Martin, or Rodney King under the permanent care and custody of governmental police agents and you begin to get the idea of what prison is.

Many young people think coming to prison is a rite of passage and they are probably right. When dad, brother, uncle, son, and grandpa have all done this same rite of passage it is hard to imagine something different. There are only two possible reasons for this sad truth. 1) The system is completely broken or 2) it is working exactly as it was designed to do. Consider carefully these words!

When I work with men in prison, one of the first things I need them to know is that the D.O.C. specifically and the prisons generally are not designed to help you. They are designed to control you. Prisons do not foster growth and success they view them as threats to security.

When we do programs, we speak about how we have been victimized and traumatized by people and events in our own lives. We come to see how these things shaped us and made us who we were. We then begin the process of healing. We stop claiming victimhood and begin to accept responsibility for our actions.

From that point forward, we begin to be in charge of our own lives. We begin to build people back up, to empower them and give them the information and insight they need to make better decisions in life. We find that core self (the inner good) and we nurture it. We encourage, empower, and support each other in trying to become better, more productive people in life. For me, this took finding my way to Buddhism and yoga. Both of them have eight limb paths of ethical conduct. In Buddhism this consists of right views, intention, speech, action, livelihood, effort, mindfulness, and concentration.

It would be a slow but steady march towards incorporation of these things in my life, but it was eventually the difference between walking a path of light instead of a path of darkness. When I teach other men, I teach with healing in mind. When I do yoga, it is with the idea of showing up in a better more positive way. Spreading positive energy rather than negative energy. The last twenty years of my life have been about healing, learning, growth and teaching. There are many people here who need healing, learning, growth, and teaching so it works out well. Whether in Spanish studies, program participation, or just talking to guys dealing with life's issues, people in prison always amaze me. They are incredibly resilient, adaptive, responsive and much more open to new concepts than I ever imagined. I have seen such incredibly damaged and broken men heal and come to believe in themselves again. I see men overcome so many obstacles in life and never quit. Not only do they never quit, they persevere, they flourish, and they thrive. It is very satisfying seeing it when it happens. Whether someone suddenly grasps an intellectual concept that has eluded them or suddenly grasps the concept that they are now in charge of their own lives is great to see. This is why I encourage people to learn. There is power in knowledge. All of these students are ready, willing and eager to learn they simply need someone to show them what they CAN do, rather than what they can't.

Please consider these words and be brave enough to see the world through fresh eyes.

Maybe something will break in my direction eventually. If and when that time comes, I want to be as prepared as possible to make the best out of what remains of my life, and to live it in a far different manner than I lived the first part.

I have been taking control of my life for many years now and continue pushing in the direction of positivity, healing and growth. If I never get out of prison, I will do the best I can with what I have. May you find it in yourself to do the same in whatever struggles you may be dealing with in life.

In the wake of getting shot down in court my dreams are pretty simple: 1) I would like some mangoes, kiwis, guava, and papaya again, 2) I would like to be able to dive into a pond during the summer, 3) I would like to take a motorcycle ride with my brother and sister up to Acadia National Park via the White Mountains of New Hampshire in the fall.

GOD GRANT ME THE SERENITY TO ACCEPT THE THINGS I CANNOT CHANGE, COURAGE TO CHANGE THE THINGS I CAN, AND THE WISDOM TO KNOW THE DIFFERENCE

God Bless

Questions to Consider

1. What are the long-term effects of a child's inability to bond with a parent? Or a parent's inability to bond with their child? Are they the same?
2. Did the author's parents correctly identify the two good kids and the two bad kids or did the cause them to be that way by parenting them differently and giving them different messages?
3. Are early educational problems a prediction of later social and emotional problems?
4. What are potential effects of pre-teen drug and alcohol problems on a child's developing brain mentally, emotionally, psychologically? Do drugs and alcohol impact maturity?
5. What differentiates childhood emotional trauma from normal growing pains?
6. What could have altered the author's self-destructive path in life, if anything? Or were his results the natural and logical conclusion to how he was living?
7. To what do you attribute the author's turnaround? Education, maturity, or spirituality?
8. Why is it important that the author accept responsibility for his crime? For his actions? For his faults?
9. Should the government incarcerate people until death to send a message that killing is wrong. Should the government really be in favor of vengeance, retribution, and vindictiveness and death? If so, why not just kill the convict. Or should the government value life, hope, redemption and re-education?
10. I believe nothing that favors death is healthy and nothing that favors life is wrong. Do you agree with this position? If not, why not?
11. If everything the author has accomplished in prison doesn't speak to redemption, then whatever would? Could the author have done more?
12. What is the value of punishment when punishment has lost its value?

To contact the author please write to;
Jeffrey A. Sinnott
MCI-Norfolk, BOX 43, Norfolk, MA. 02056

Author today

Out in California

My sister Val and I

Summer before disaster

Missing out on family traditions with Denise, Jon, Val, and Jon's wife Cheryl

Missing out on my Father's passing (Denise, Jon, Val)

Historical House on Mower St where I grew up.

Christmas at Norfolk

Still able to smile and stay positive

Eyes are going from so much reading

At the prison with my mom

Discipline wasn't enough to save me from myself

Trying to become a better person

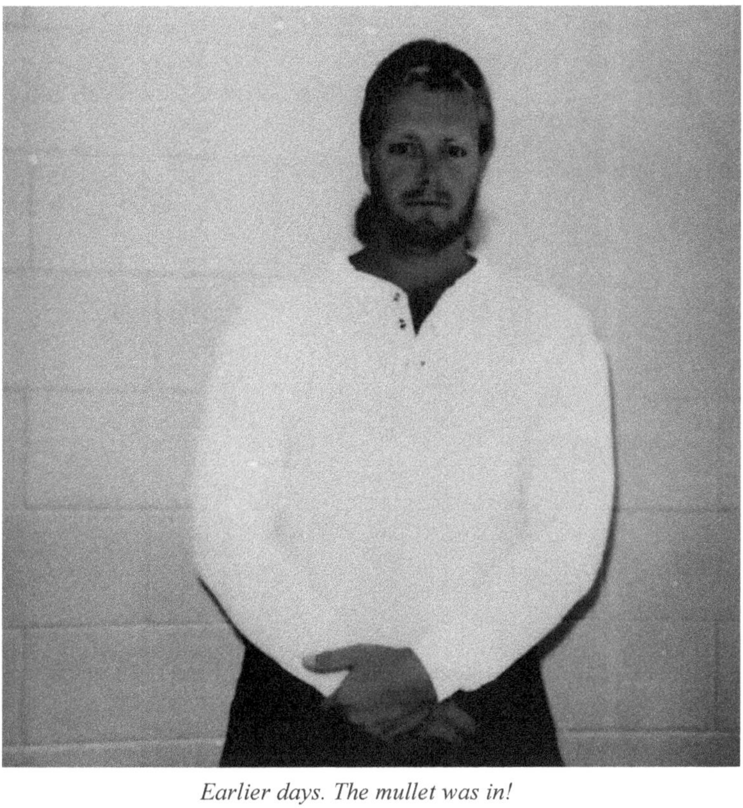

Earlier days. The mullet was in!

Dad, me getting my first degree, my grandmother, and my mom

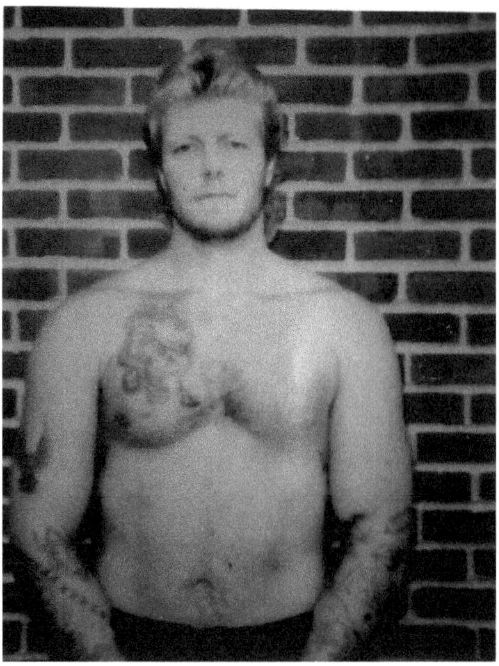

Trying to stay alive

Val, Denise, Mom, Me at grandma's for Christmas

Printed in the USA
CPSIA information can be obtained
at www.ICGtesting.com
LVHW070158231024
794592LV00010B/38

9 798887 293868